Freedom: Living Above Your Circumstance

T. K. Anderson

*"For we speak as messengers approved by God to be **entrusted** with the Good News. Our purpose is to please God, not people."* 1 Thess. 2:4

Entrusted Ministries
Scottsdale, Arizona

Published by Entrusted Ministries
Scottsdale, Arizona (USA)

Acknowledgments:
Editing: Daniel Johnson
Interior Design: Karen Stuart
Cover Design: David Landis

©2022, T.K. Anderson; *Freedom: Living Above Your Circumstance*

All rights reserved.
No part of this book may be used or reproduced in any manner whatsoever without written permission except in the case of brief quotations embodied in critical articles, Bible studies, sermons, and reviews.

First edition softcover: November 2022
First edition eBook: November 2022

Printed in the United States of America

Dedication

This book is dedicated to those who have faced challenges, struggles, and adversity beyond belief. You are the ones who have inspired so many. Like the Apostle Paul, through Christ, you have risen above your circumstance and have encouraged me.

Especially to my sister, who, at a young age, faced one of life's most difficult challenges. I'll never forget your faith in Christ as you overcame and continue to trust in the sovereignty of God. You have lived out this powerful biblical truth –

"For our light and momentary troubles are achieving for us an eternal glory that far outweighs them all."

2 Corinthians 4:17

Contents

Introduction 7

Part One: Free to Live in Christ - A look at *Ephesians*

    Chapter One - Live in Grace (2:8-10) 15

    Chapter Two - Live in Unity (4:1-3) 33

    Chapter Three - Live in Power (6:10-18) 51

Interlude: Journey from Ephesians to Philippians 73

Part Two: Free to Rejoice through Christ - A look at *Philippians*

    Chapter Four: Rejoice in Hardship (1:12-26) 77

    Chapter Five: Rejoice in Humility (2:1-11) 103

    Chapter Six: Rejoice in Citizenship (3:12-21) 125

Interlude: Journey from Philippians to Colossians 149

Part Three: Free to Trust in Christ – A look at *Colossians*

    Chapter Seven: Trust in His Royalty (1:15-20) 153

    Chapter Eight: Trust in His Redemption (2:6-15) 177

    Chapter Nine: Trust in His Restoration (3:1-17) 201

Interlude: Journey from Colossians to Philemon 219

Part Four: Free to Forgive because of Christ - A look at *Philemon*

    Chapter Ten: Why Forgiveness is so Powerful 223

Finale 241

About the Author 247

Endnotes 249

T.K. Anderson

Introduction

Imagine for a moment you are in the darkest of situations through no fault of your own. In fact, you were doing nothing more than minding your own business while deeply involved in activities that brought joy and happiness to thousands of people. You were being welcomed by the humblest citizens and noblest leaders. Yet at a moment's notice, you find yourself locked up and locked down. You have been silenced by forces beyond your control.

This is what happened in 58 A.D. to a man named Saul of Tarsus. By the time of his unfortunate capture, he was being referred to by Christians as the apostle Paul. But to others who knew his history, he was no apostle. This was Saul. How dare he change his name to hide his past. He was nothing more than a nuisance to the public and heretic to the old way of religious understanding. He was a fly to be swatted. A flea to be removed. He was to be jailed, stopped, tried, and convicted. It seemed all was lost for Paul.

Similarly, on Saturday, December 17, 1927, the crew of the Navy submarine USS S-4 was surfacing from a run off the waters of Cape Cod Bay. They were engaged in routine testing of their vessel. The Coast Guard Cutter, Paulding, was traveling across the surface doing the same. The vessels never saw each other. The submarine broke the surface just in time to receive a death blow from the Paulding. The submarine with its crew of forty sank in less than five minutes. It came to rest more than one hundred feet below on the ocean floor.

Rescue attempts, though meager and primitive in 1927, began at once. Due to impossible weather, it took twenty-four hours for the first diver to descend to the wreckage. As soon as the diver's feet hit the hull, he heard tapping. There were survivors, alive, trapped inside.

Pounding out Morse code on the hull with a hammer, the diver discovered six crewmen had survived the collision. Efforts were renewed to reach these men before it was too late. But again, the weather would not cooperate. Every attempt at salvation failed.

With their air supply dwindling, the six survivors tapped out in Morse code a final haunting question, "Is there any hope?" For the crew of the S-4, hope would not come soon enough. It was three months before the Navy sent the necessary pontoons to raise the vessel.[1]

What do you do when you find yourself in a hopeless situation? How do you handle it when the tide has turned on you? When you find yourself in an oppressive situation? When those in authority want to silence your voice, what can be done? None of us is immune to trying circumstances. We have all faced moments when everything seemed lost. When our ship has sunk, and the air is running low. Perhaps at that moment, you felt as though God abandoned you too. It is not uncommon for us to think and feel this way.

Thankfully amid his darkness, the apostle Paul refused to allow the light of God's presence to be snuffed out. Religious rulers of his day wanted to silence his voice, and they did, but only for a brief moment. What ensued from his imprisonment was four letters we still have today. Instead of silencing his voice, they gave voice to the letters we know as the prison epistles.

We live in a broken world with broken people, and because of

Freedom

this brokenness, many of us find ourselves imprisoned by the events of life. I want to share with you that there is hope, there is an escape, and there is freedom to be found. Not only from life's circumstances, but as we go through life's circumstances.

I have never been in a physical jail, except for brief moments of ministry when it felt like it. I cannot imagine what being in prison would be like. But I have felt the prison-like bars of oppression before. I have felt the heavy-handedness of persecution, the pain of a lost family member, the deep desolation of doubt, and the hurt of betrayal. None of it is enjoyable, yet none of has to be final.

I invite you to join me as we journey back in time when the apostle Paul found himself in a hopeless situation but refused to allow the oppressiveness to dictate his response. As we journey, consider this story from over 200 years ago that illustrates the beauty found within the hardest struggles we may have.

In 1799, Conrad Reed discovered a seventeen-pound rock while fishing in Little Meadow Creek. Not knowing what it was made of his family used it as a doorstop for three years. In 1802, his father, John Reed, took it to a jeweler who identified it as a lump of gold worth about $3,600. That lump of gold, which was used as a doorstop for three years in North Carolina, is one of the biggest gold nuggets ever found east of the Rockies.

Until its composition was determined, its value was unknown. Likewise, until the composition of our faith is determined, its strength is unknown. God allows trials in our lives not to hurt us, but to strengthen and prove us.[2]

What exactly are the prison epistles? The word, *epistle,* is another word for a *letter.* The prison letters, then, are a collection of tailor-made messages to emerging Christian congregations in the Mediterranean towns of Ephesus, Philippi, and Colossae. One of these personalized letters was written to a man named, Philemon, in the city of Colossae.

We find these cities first mentioned in Acts within chapters sixteen through eighteen. Paul made initial contact with these locations during his second missionary journey. In Acts chapter twenty-one through twenty-eight, we find Paul's arrest in Jerusalem and imprisoned sailing journey to Rome.

It was in Rome during his house arrest, between the years 60 and 62 A.D., that he wrote these four influential letters. We find in Acts 28:16, that while under house arrest Paul was guarded by soldiers, was permitted to host visitors, shared the gospel, and influenced members of Caesar's household. (Philippians 4:22)

The four letters are pastoral in nature. Throughout the texts, you can sense a shepherd's heart for his flock. Paul's mind is first-rate, yet it is his heart for the Body of Christ that permeates the text. Each letter has a specific emphasis for each congregation. Nevertheless, they are tied together through a unified message of Christ and his kingdom being lived out through the people of God. Let's take a quick snapshot of each book.

Paul wrote Ephesians to explain some of the great doctrines of the faith in chapters one through three. He spells out the important doctrines of Christian behavior in chapters four through six. Ephesus was an abundant and influential city during the first century. The Bible tells us Paul spent a great deal of time there. He was very interested in keeping his prominent Aegean Sea location secure.

He begins his letter by addressing it to, "the saints in Ephesus." (1:1) His main emphasis was to help establish the gospel as being universal in extent. His main theme was simple; the kingdom of God is here and will continue throughout eternity. This was the big picture for Paul, and he wanted to bring the Ephesians along with him. As he did that, he also explained how they could live out their faith within their current society.

Philippians was written as an encouragement to be joyful regardless of the situation, even in the midst of suffering. The following nine passages highlight this point: 1:4, 1:18, 1:25-26, 2:2, 2:28, 3:1, 4:1, 4:4, and 4:10. Epaphroditus, a member of the church at Philippi, brought supplies from Philippi to Paul while he was imprisoned at Rome. (Philippians 2:25 and 4:18) He had a serious illness while in Rome. He was loved by both Paul and the Philippians. (Philippians 2:25-30) On his return home, Epaphroditus delivered the epistle to the church in Philippi.

Colossians was written to defeat false teaching in the church. (1:15-20 and 2:2-10, 2:11-23) The theme of Colossians is the all-inclusive sufficiency of Christ as compared to the void of mere human philosophy or religious routines. Epaphras most likely founded the church in Colossae and worked among the churches of Laodicea and Hierapolis. Paul calls Epaphras a "faithful minister." (1:7, 4:12-13, Acts 19:10)

Paul never explicitly describes the false teaching he opposes in the Colossian letter. The nature of the heresy must be inferred from statements he made in opposition to the false teachers. It is likely the Colossian heresy was a mixture of an extreme form of Judaism and an early stage of Gnosticism.

Philemon was written as a plea for forgiveness to his fellow worker and house church leader on behalf of his new friend, Onesimus. The book is only one chapter with twenty-five verses in total or 335 words in the original Greek. Onesimus, a slave, who after robbing his master, Philemon, at Colossae, fled to Rome. There he was converted by the apostle Paul, who sent him back to his master with the epistle which bears his name. In it, he asks Philemon to receive his slave as a "faithful and beloved brother." Paul offers to pay Philemon anything his slave had taken, and to bear the wrong he had done him. He was accompanied on his return by Tychicus, the bearer of the Epistle to the Colossians. (Philemon 1:16,18)

The story of this fugitive Colossian slave is remarkable evidence of the freedom of access to Paul. It is also a beautiful illustration both of the character of Paul and the transforming power and great principles of the gospel. Paul's plea was for Onesimus to be profitable for the Gospel. (1:11)

Philemon pardoned him and set him free, and Onesimus returned to Paul as Paul requested (21). He faithfully served and we know Paul made Onesimus, with Tychicus, the bearer of this epistle to the Colossians (Col.4:7-9). Later, Jerome and other Church Fathers indicate, Onesimus became a dedicated minister of the gospel and a bishop. He followed Timothy as bishop of Ephesus. He was tortured in Rome. His martyrdom occurred under the Roman emperor, Domitian, in the year 95 A.D.

As followers of Christ, we too face obstacles in living out our faith every day. There are times we feel isolated from other Christians and alone in this journey. We ask ourselves, **"How do we live out this Christian experience effectively every single day?"**

Freedom

There are times we desperately avoid struggle because we are afraid of its damaging effects. We wonder, *"How can I find joy in the middle of all I'm going through?"*

Other times we feel as though trust is something nonexistent in this world and cannot be found in anyone. *"How can I trust when everything around me is broken and untrustworthy?"*

Lastly, when we have been wounded by others we ask, *"How do I find the strength to forgive when I cannot find the way to forgive, or I do not feel like it?"*

These four questions and more are answered in Paul's prison letters. In sum, although a prisoner of Rome, in Paul's mind, his captivity was first to Christ.[3] I am glad you have joined in on the journey.

Let's get started.

T.K. Anderson

Chapter One

Live in Grace

Ephesians 2:8-10

After twenty years of shaving himself every morning, a man in a small Southern town decided he had enough. He told his wife he intended to let the local barber shave him each day. He put on his hat and coat and went to the barbershop, which was owned by the pastor of the town's Baptist Church.

The barber's wife, Grace, was working that day, so she performed the task. Grace shaved him and sprayed him with lilac water, and said, "That will be $20." The man thought the price was a bit high, but he paid the bill and went to work.

The next morning the man looked in the mirror, and his face was as smooth as it had been when he left the barber shop the day before. "Not bad," he thought. "At least I don't need to get a shave every day." The next morning, the man's face was still smooth. Two weeks later, the man was still unable to find any trace of whiskers on his face. It was more than he could take, so he returned to the barbershop.

"I thought $20 was high for a shave," he told the barber's wife, "but you must have done a great job. It's been two weeks and my whiskers still haven't started growing back."

Her expression didn't change as she was expecting his

comment. She responded, "You were shaved by Grace and once shaved, always shaved!"[4]

So, what is grace from God's perspective? What does it mean to be saved by grace? When we use the word *grace* we often think of forgiveness, to pardon or be nice to someone. But is that what grace means from a biblical perspective?

In Paul's four prison letters he addresses this all-important issue. He gives special attention to the topic in the first half of his first letter to the Christians in Ephesus. But what exactly do we know about his letter, Ephesians?

Paul writes his all-important letter not only to the believers in Ephesus but also those in nearby cities of the Lycus Valley. Cities such as Laodicea, Colossae, and Hierapolis. How do we know this? There are hints within the letter indicating Paul had not yet met some of his readers. (1:15 & 3:2-3) Additionally, we know Paul's friend, Tychicus, delivered at least two of Paul's four letters. (Eph 6:21-22 & Col 4:7-8) Tychicus most likely delivered both letters (*Ephesians/Colossians*) on the same trip and distributed them equally, or in pairs.

The purpose of Ephesians was to address several challenges in terms of God's Kingdom. Paul's general motif was that through Christ, the kingdom of God had now been established on earth. We are living out this last phase until the return of Christ, which will at that time, usher in the rule and reign of Christ upon our planet. We see this future reign described in Revelation chapter 20 and other prophetic passages, as the millennial reign of Christ.

We notice a two-part thought in Paul's teaching in Acts 28:30-31, as Luke captures Paul's mindset while writing his four prison letters. Luke records, *"30 For two whole years Paul stayed there [under house arrest in Rome] in his own rented house and welcomed all who came to see him. 31 He proclaimed the kingdom of God and taught about the Lord Jesus Christ—with all boldness and without hindrance!"*

Paul taught that the gospel (the "Good News") and the kingdom of God were in play now but would be fully revealed to believers in the future. He taught freedom and the future, all bound up within the grace of God.

In the first three chapters of Ephesians, Paul emphasizes some of the great doctrines of the church. In the middle of these three chapters, a famous set of verses in the Book of Ephesians chapter two capture for us the concept of grace and what it means today. *"8 For by grace you have been saved through faith. 9 And this is not your own doing; it is the gift of God, not a result of works, so that no one may boast. 10 For we are his workmanship, created in Christ Jesus for good works, which God prepared beforehand, that we should walk in them."*

Here is an interesting Bible detail for you: The total number of words in the first half of Ephesians (which includes chapters one through three) is 1,400. In chapter two, verse ten, the two-word phrase, *in Christ,* is the precise hinge point of the first half of Ephesians – 700 words before and 700 words after. If you ever doubt where our theology rests, or better yet, in *whom* our theology rests, Paul wants you to know, it is in Christ.

It is in Christ that we have the greatest promise in all our theology, which is salvation. God reached down, walked among us, and by grace provided a way to reconnect with those He foreknew and predestined to receive this great news. To live in grace then is to understand the plan, praise, and purpose of salvation as Paul clearly explains in this pivotal set of verses. Let us start with the plan of salvation.

The Plan of Salvation

"For by grace you have been saved through faith." Eph 2:8

Here we see the cause, effect, and mechanism. Grace is the cause. Salvation is the effect. Faith is the mechanism. In the first part of this passage, we see Paul laying out the clear plan of salvation for us. It is by grace we have been saved, he writes, and yet it is through faith as well. If you are like me, you have at least three questions for Paul:

- Where is grace coming from and how do I get it?
- What am I being saved from?
- Where or in whom do I put my faith to secure salvation?

If this is God's strategy, I want to know how it works. How about you?

Former President Ronald Reagan says he learned the need for having a strategy early in life. An aunt had taken him to a cobbler to have a pair of shoes made. The shoemaker asked him, "Do you want a square toe or a round toe?" Reagan hemmed and hawed. So, the cobbler said, "Come back in a day or two and let me know what you want." A few days later the shoemaker saw Reagan on the street and asked what he had decided about the shoes. "I still haven't made up my mind," the boy answered. "Very well," said the cobbler.

When Reagan finally received the shoes, he was shocked to see one shoe had a square toe and the other a round toe. "Looking at those shoes every day taught me a lesson," he said. Years later, Regan commented, "If you don't make your own decisions, somebody else will make them for you!"[5]

Thankfully, God decided a long time ago about us and created a strategy to save us instead of putting it off like the young Ronald Reagan.

We know from the text that we are saved by grace. But what exactly is grace? Simply put, it is God's favor upon us. It means God has favored us, or in today's language, God has privileged us. What does it feel like to be favored by God? It might feel like what Mary the mother of Jesus felt.

The angel, Gabriel, appeared and told Mary she was going to carry the Son of God in her womb. She was perplexed and afraid. The Bible records this account in Luke 1:30, *"And the angel said to her, "Do not be afraid, Mary, for you have found favor with God."* That word *favor* is the same word Paul used in Ephesians 2:8. It's a Greek word, *charis* (khä'-res χάρις), and it means to have God "benefit or privilege" your life.

Luke 2:40 refers to this quality in the life of Jesus when he was a little boy, *"And the child grew and became strong, filled with wisdom. And the favor of God was upon him."* Again, it is the same word, *charis* (khä'-res χάρις).

Luke again uses the same word Paul used for grace in Acts 2:46-47 when he writes, *"[46] And day by day, attending the temple together and breaking bread in their homes, they received their food with glad and generous hearts, [47] praising God and having favor with all the people. And the Lord added to their number day by day those who were being saved."*

When we put this together, we can clearly see that grace is much more than being nice or doing a favor for someone. Sometimes it is that. But in Paul's case, it means having favor bestowed upon us. As a Christian, it means God has bestowed his favor upon our entire life. That is what Paul is getting across here with this little three-word phrase, "For by grace."

It means that without God's favor upon us, we are lost. We are dead in our sins and completely cut off for all of eternity. This is a tough message. This is a sober thought. We live in an independent culture. A culture of individual choice and personal freedom. Yet Paul is explaining that our connection to God is not by our choice alone. We do not get to "just choose" God. He has to first provide favor to us and aid our decision-making process.

A.W. Tozer writes, "Grace is the good pleasure of God that inclines Him to bestow benefits upon the undeserving. Its usage to us sinful men is to save us and make us sit together in heavenly places to demonstrate to the ages the exceeding riches of God's kindness to us in Christ Jesus."[6]

The answer, then, to our first question for Paul is that grace comes from God and is given by God. There is nothing you or I can do to purchase it, inherit it, deserve it, demand it, or coerce God into providing it. His grace, favor, or privilege is from him and by him alone. That means we cannot mess it up, lose it, misplace it, evade it, or elude its pull on our life. When God gives us his favor, we cannot stop it. That is why the gospel is called "good news."

So, if you are feeling a bit down or lost, or feel like you are a million miles from God, can I encourage you that if you are hearing or reading this message that means God's favor is on your life. He wants you to know and understand the meaning of salvation,

Freedom

otherwise, you would not be hearing or reading this message.

Listen, friend, God is for you. You have the favor of God on your life. That should encourage you. God has not given up on you, so do not give up on yourself. This is the core message to the believers in Ephesus and the core message for us today.

Dr. David Jeremiah writes, "Paul mentions grace twelve times in this letter as he declares God's calling and purpose for every believer. He catalogs God's many rich blessings through Christ – blessings that should strengthen every Christian's confidence and endurance."[7]

Now that we know God's grace is upon us, according to the text in verse eight, what precisely are we being saved from?

A young girl accepted Christ as her Savior and applied for membership in a local church. "Were you a sinner before you received the Lord Jesus into your life?" inquired an old deacon. "Yes sir," she replied. "Well, are you still a sinner?" He asked.

"To tell you the truth, I feel I'm a greater sinner than ever," she replied.

"Then what real change have you experienced?" Asked the deacon.

"I don't quite know how to explain it," the young girl said, "except I used to be a sinner running after sin, but now that I am saved. I'm a sinner running from sin!"[8]

The Bible is clear: We all suffer from the same two problems. All the wisdom or resources in the world cannot remove these two problems. That is our battle with sin, and the ability to overcome our final death. The good news is the resurrection of Jesus Christ

T.K. Anderson

takes care of these two problems.

Sin? Not an issue anymore. I paid the price for you, Jesus says.

Death? Not a problem, it has been conquered.

Paul comments on this very thing in Colossians 2:13-15, *[13]And you, who were dead in your trespasses…God made alive together with him, having forgiven us all our trespasses, [14] by canceling the record of debt that stood against us with its legal demands. This he set aside, nailing it to the cross. [15] He disarmed the rulers and authorities and put them to open shame, by triumphing over them in him."*

The third part of this opening point is that it's "through faith" in Christ, Paul writes, that secures the blessings of salvation for us. And we base that on the passage we just read in Colossians chapter two. Our redemption is secured by the atoning work of Christ at Calvary.

So, what's the mechanism to receive this salvation from God? It's faith. Faith is another word for trust. Let me ask you, have you put your trust in Christ? If not, why not?

Listen, if you have a personal failure, daunting question, or unresolved issue, let me tell you… Welcome to the club! We all do. Don't let that keep you from putting your full trust in Christ. Allow me to tell you what I've discovered. As you put your faith in him, you will uncover that many of those intimidating questions fade away. Many of those unresolved issues get resolved over time.

And once you understand God's grace and love for you, those personal failures move from the foreground to the background and eventually below ground, dead and buried with your old nature in the grave where they belong. God's plan of salvation can be summarized as God's favor, plus nothing, through Christ, equals redemption and new life.

2 Corinthians 5:17, *"Therefore, if anyone is in Christ, he is a new creation. The old has passed away; behold, the new has come."*

The first thing we need to do to live by grace is to understand God's plan of salvation. Now, let's look at the second thing to understand as we learn to live by grace. Who gets the credit for this great salvation? Paul addresses this in the next section of the text. It's found in the praise of salvation.

The Praise for Salvation

8"And this is not your own doing; it is the gift of God, 9not a result of works, so that no one may boast." Ephesians 2:8-9

Here's what Paul is saying: First of all, this is not from the mind of mankind! This is not your own doing; it is the gift of God. You didn't come up with this plan of salvation. This isn't, wasn't, and never could have been your idea. Paul is saying, "You may be creative, but you're not that creative!"

When the Cornerstone Bank in Waco, Nebraska, was robbed of some $6,000 in November of 2012, the bank employees were able to give the police a fairly good description of the teenage girl who pulled off the crime, and the car in which she escaped. As it turned out, the investigators didn't need those descriptions because the thief recorded a YouTube video titled, "Chick Bank Robber," boasting of her criminal know-how.

Fanning out the cash in front of the camera, 19-year-old Hannah Sabata held up a sign that read, "I just stole a car and robbed a bank. Now I'm rich, I can pay off my college financial aid, and tomorrow I'm going for a shopping spree." Later she held up another sign which said, "I told my mom today was the best day of my life." Hannah's brief criminal career ended later that week when police took her into custody.[9]

As clever and creative as we may think we are, we're really no different than Hannah Sabata when it comes to trying to figure out a way to escape from the consequences of our offense before a holy God. We think we've pulled it off and now we're on easy street. We may even brag or boast about it. This isn't a new occurrence. Humans have always tried to create some type of rescue plan to get us out of this jam with our Creator.

Peter addresses this issue in his second letter, *"For we did not follow cleverly devised myths when we made known to you the power and coming of our Lord Jesus Christ."* (2 Peter 1:16) Peter is agreeing with Paul in saying that the gospel is not some story thought up in the mind of mankind like all the other religious systems and structures in the world. Peter is saying this is different and he is an eyewitness of the whole deal.

If we think about it, historical evidence agrees with what Peter and Paul are saying here. In fact, within all religious structures known to man, it's always man doing something to merit God's blessing in return for something done on behalf of the deity. Without exception, from the mind of mankind, we develop a self-made salvation from us to God.

God is telling us the exact opposite in this passage. He is saying this isn't from you, it's from me. From the mind of God, from the heart of God, and not from your cleverness or creativity.

Secondly, Paul is saying this is not from the works of mankind!

He is saying that you can't earn it, even if you try. This gift of salvation isn't from your mind and it's not from your hands. Some may do better than others, but we all fall short. Let's say we're sailing to Hawaii and our boat goes down halfway there. Some may go down with the ship, some may swim a few miles, and some may even make it a day or two, but the reality is, we all will fall short, and we all will perish. God is saying to us, you can't earn this, and you can't design this because the ocean is too vast, and you don't know how to handle the coming storms.

When the massive Hurricane Charley slammed into Florida in 2004 with 145 mile-per-hour winds, it destroyed more than 12,000 homes. But a later study by a group of insurance companies found that almost all of those homes had something in common—they had been built prior to 2001. In that year, a strict new building code was adopted which required homes to be strengthened to withstand hurricane-force winds.

Jeff Burton, building code manager for the Institute for Business and Home Safety said, "There is very, very strong evidence that buildings built under the 2001 code that were built properly and inspected...fared much, much better than buildings that were built prior. The building code, as it exists today, did its job."[10]

The Bible tells us God set up a new covenant when Christ came to the earth and died on the cross for your sins. In essence, he instituted a new code. If you and I continue to operate under the old code of the law, sacrificial systems, or religious structures, when the storm of judgment day arrives, we will be crushed. There is a reason for the new building code, and those who follow it find that it works.

And why? So, we can't boast about it. None of us can boast

about what God has done for us. None of us has arrived. None of us can say to the others among us, if you were only a bit more like me then there would be hope for you. Pride comes before the fall, the Bible tells us. (Proverbs 16:18) Once we've been lifted up from our sins, God doesn't want us to fall again into the very pride from which he's redeemed us.

Now that we've learned about the plan and praise for salvation, let's take a look at the purpose of salvation. Why does God reach his hand down to planet earth and redeem us? For what purpose, what's the point?

The Purpose of Salvation

"For we are his workmanship, created in Christ Jesus for good works, which God prepared beforehand, that we should walk in them." Ephesians 2:10

Now we get to the last and best part. God doesn't save us, set us apart, and protect us from our pride just so he can put us in some type of heavenly museum one day. Nope, he saves us for the express purpose of "doing good works" for him. Which, by the way, he prepared in advance for us to do.

This word, *workmanship,* is from the Greek word poiēma (poi'-a-mä) and is used in only two verses in the entire Bible, here and in Romans 1:20. *"For his invisible attributes, namely, his eternal power and divine nature, have been clearly perceived, ever since he creation of the world, in the 'things that have been made'(poi'-a-mä). So, they are without excuse."*

Paul is saying, as we "walk in good works, prepared in advance for us to do," it's just as important to God's creative order as the marvelous creation all around us. We may say to someone, "Look

Freedom

up at the night sky and in the huge expanse of the universe you can see the handiwork of God." "Do you see God's creative power?" we might ask. And yet, Paul is saying the same here, in Ephesians 2:10, about our lives. As we walk in the good works Christ has prepared for us to accomplish, we become a testimony to the eternal power and divine nature of God.

But how would that work in a practical sense? Using the Ephesians as our example, Max Anders in his Holman New Testament Commentary helps us to see the practical side of how early Christians impacted their culture in such an amazing fashion. Something remarkable happened in the cities, towns, and villages in which the gospel was preached. Jews and Gentiles began to worship together. They began to share resources. They began to exhibit unity as the Body of Christ. They became a living example of Christ to the world.

Regarding this impact in Ephesus, Anders writes, "We [simply] do not understand the degree of separation that existed between Jews and Gentiles. It is like saying there will no longer be blacks and whites in South Africa. It is like saying there will be no longer Catholics and Protestants in Ireland. It is like saying there will no longer be liberals and conservatives in the United States. All these people are going to be made into one."[11]

This thought regarding Christian impact in Ephesus is expanded, "In Paul's day, the animosity between Jew and Gentile was so strong that a Jewish woman would not help a Gentile woman deliver her child because the Jewish woman believed she was helping to bring another degraded human into the world. Jews would not even go through Samaria because it was a non-Jewish country. They would walk 150 miles out of their way – around the border – to keep from entering territory inhabited by a people they called 'dogs.' So when the gospel offered grace to all, it produced a massive shift. Suddenly, there could be no separate Jewish church, no separate Gentile church. God had only one family – and Jew and Gentile alike had equal status. It was a truly revolutionary time in the church."[12]

This is what Paul meant when he said *"we should walk in"* these good works *"prepared in advance"* for us to do by Christ. When we join together and break down the barriers and walls between us, it's an example to the world of Christ breaking down the wall of sin, between us and God. We offer forgiveness because we are forgiven. We offer favor because we have been favored. We offer acceptance because we are accepted.

This same word, (poi'-a-mä) is also where we get the English word poem from. We are God's poem as the Body of Christ to live out his story to those around us.

Finally, think on this for a moment... these good works (we are to do) aren't necessarily limited to this temporal "kingdom of man" as we are living in now. Expand our mind for a moment, as a Christian how far into the future has Christ prepared in advance for you? Do these "good works" include the Millennial reign? The Bible is clear in that we will be ruling and reigning with Christ during that time frame. And Paul emphasized this idea many times in his writing: The Kingdom of God is now here and continues to extend past this temporal kingdom of the current age. So, this should give us even something to ponder and even more be looking forward to as followers of Christ.

So now, go walk in those good works prepared in advance for you to do today!

Conclusion

Recalling that Paul wrote this letter to the believers in Ephesus, as he was under house arrest, he is reminding us that even though we may be surrounded by oppression we have freedom, within that oppression, to enjoy the gifts of God for us. The chief of those gifts is salvation through Christ. Paul's letter serves to remind us that to live in grace is to understand the plan, praise, and purpose of salvation.

We started out by learning that the plan of salvation is based upon accepting God's love for us. God's plan of salvation can be summarized as God's favor, plus nothing, through Christ, equals redemption and new life. Have you accepted his love for you yet?

We then came to appreciate the praise for salvation is owed to Christ. This plan of redemption is not from the mind of man nor the hand of man, but rather rests solely upon the work of Christ upon Calvary. Have you thanked him for redeeming you lately?

And lastly, we discovered that the purpose of our salvation is not to be put upon some heavenly shelf in a celestial museum one day after we die, but rather it's to live out the very nature of Christ right now. We have been designed by God to be the very image of Christ through our actions every day. Are you living out those "good works" prepared in advance by Christ, each day?

I can hear some say to this, "That's fine for you, but you don't know my life. I'm in a deep fog and my life is a wreck. I can't seem to catch a break and everything I try seems to end up broken, destroyed, or ruined." Listen, friend, I don't know everything you've been through or may be going through, but I know the One who can help you through it.

T.K. Anderson

Come to Christ afresh today. Don't wait. He's been calling you to himself, that's why you're reading this today. If he didn't want to speak to you this very moment you wouldn't be here, you'd be doing something else. Sadly, many people wait or postpone giving their life over to Christ. Not only do they completely miss out on what God has for this life, for some it becomes entirely too late for the life to come as well.

On Easter Sunday, 2013, the southbound side of I-77 near the North Carolina-Virginia border was closed for hours following a massive chain of accidents. Police later reported that seventeen different collisions involved ninety-five cars and trucks. The wrecks left three people dead, and more than two dozen injured, many of them seriously. The cause of the accidents was people driving into a thick fog that descended over the Interstate that Sunday afternoon. A police spokesman said, "Visibility at the time this accident occurred was down to about one hundred feet or less." As people continued to drive blindly forward, they could not see the danger that was just ahead until it was too late.[13]

Maybe that story's a metaphor for your life right now. You've crashed, you're banged up and broken down. Well, you have a few choices. You can sit around and wonder how it all happened and think about all the things that went wrong. You can blame the fog, the people in front of you, the manufacturer of the vehicle, or a host of other things. Or you can bring your life to Christ, just as you are, broken, battered, and bruised and he will pick you up, heal your wounds and get you back on the path he originally intended. He'll put you on a new road called the Narrow Road. The roads on his highway are well paved, contain no tolls, and I can assure you, aren't covered in fog.

For others, maybe this chapter is a clarion call for you to pull your life over today before it's too late. God is saying, "Stop driving into the fog, danger awaits you!" If you know you're on the road to destruction, can I appeal for you to pull over now, turn around and head back?

Matthew 7:13: *"Enter through the narrow gate. For wide is the gate and broad is the road that leads to destruction, and many enter through it."*

Either way, whichever situation you find yourself in today, it's time to live in grace. Open your heart to Christ today and begin to enjoy all that he has planned for you and all that he's prepared in advance for you. He does all of this so that you can be an impact for his kingdom and his glory.

T.K. Anderson

Chapter Two

Live in Unity

Ephesians 4:1-3

In his book, *A Life Beyond Amazing,* Dr. David Jeremiah tells a gripping story demonstrating the power and cost of unity found among a group of individuals.[14] He writes, "On October 22, 2007, the first Medal of Honor awarded for combat in Afghanistan was presented to the family of Lt. Michael Murphy, a Navy SEAL who gave his life to make a radio call for help for his team. Murphy, who was not yet thirty, was only the fourth Navy SEAL to earn the Medal of Honor since the Vietnam War.

In June 2005, Murphy and three other SEALs were sent on a mission into the rugged Afghan mountains to search for a known terrorist. They encountered local tribesmen who reported them to the Taliban. Murphy's team was trapped by scores of enemy troops who surrounded them on three sides and forced them into a ravine. Soon all four men had sustained injuries. "We were hurtin,'" said the team's sole survivor, Petty Officer 2nd Class Marcus Luttrell. "We were out of ammo, and…it was bad, it was real bad."

Murphy moved from man to man to keep his team together, though he had to expose himself to enemy fire to do so. Then, because the mountainous terrain blocked communications, he decided to move into an open area to call for help. Already wounded, and despite incoming fire, he provided his unit's location and information about the opposing force. While making the call, he took two more rounds and dropped the handset but managed to retrieve it and complete the call. He even said thank you at the end of the transmission.[15]

Petty officer Luttrell survived the firestorm because he was blasted over the ridge by a rocket-propelled grenade and was knocked unconscious. When he came to, he hid in a rock crevice, staunching his bleeding wounds with mud. Almost a week later, after being taken in by local villagers who refused to turn him over to the Taliban, he was rescued.

Marcus Luttrell came home determined to tell the story of that day. His book, *Lone Survivor*, became a movie of the same name, ensuring that Lt. Michael Murphy and the rest of his team are never forgotten."

Wouldn't it be wonderful if Christians protected each other with this same sort of commitment as these soldiers? Imagine what kind of ministry we could accomplish in our communities if we bound together as believers, especially with those who are under some type of attack. The Bible tells us we're better together than when we are apart. But do we really believe that? If we do, then why is being unified such a difficult thing to do?

After spending the first half of his letter to the Ephesians laying out major doctrines of the church, Paul now shifts his topic to a scholarly "*how to*" seminar in regard to living out our Christian experience. Starting in chapter four, and through chapter six, Paul covers the following major themes: unity in the body of Christ, personal lifestyle choices, proper family relationships, and spiritual warfare. He does all of this for the expressed purpose of building up the Church.

There is a danger to division, Paul knows this, and he reminds the leaders of Ephesus to avoid discord and seek to stay unified. Paul also knows that keeping unity requires work, and it's embedded within a proper understanding of what it takes to be a Christian. To that end, he provides a three-step outline for us to follow so that we can achieve unity and enjoy the freedom it provides.

Let's take a look at Ephesians 4:1-3. In these three verses, we find three principles that can be applied to our lives today in our search to be unified.

First, he encourages us to seek unity with each other based on our individual walk with Christ. He then lays out four characteristics that help maintain unity within the body. Finally, he concludes with a picture describing the patchwork of our divine connection. Let's start first with the quest for unity.

The Quest for Unity

"*I, therefore, a prisoner for the Lord, urge you to walk in a manner worthy of the calling to which you have been called.*" Ephesians 4:1

Paul starts out the second half of his letter with a personal call to the Ephesians to think about their individual lives before discussing this concept of corporate unity. He does so with urgency in his voice when he writes, *"I urge you to walk worthy."* Paul is on a quest to live as Christ, and he imparts to the Ephesians this same passion.

We see this in Philippians 1:21, *"For to me to **live is Christ**, and to **die is gain**."* And I Corinthians 11:1, *"Be **imitators of me**, as **I am of Christ**."* And this phrase, **"walk worthy"** is a theme in his other prison letters too.

Look at Philippians 1:27, *"Only let your manner of life be worthy of the gospel of Christ, so that whether I come and see you or am absent, I may hear of you that you are standing firm in one spirit, with one mind striving side by side for the faith of the gospel."*

And Colossians 1:10, *"so as to walk in a manner worthy of the Lord, fully pleasing to him: bearing fruit in every good work and increasing in the knowledge of God"*

The idea here is to walk or live in a way that shows or displays the weight of God's transformative effect upon my life. Worthy means, weight as in comparison to something, like a balance to the other side of the scale. The literal definition is to be something that "draws down the scale."

The question for us is; Do I live in a way that corresponds to the high position I have as a child of God? If not, Paul is urging us to make a change so that it does. But isn't that a bit harsh for Paul to be telling the Ephesians to step it up a bit? What if they don't like receiving correction in their life? Who gives him the right to be telling them to walk worthy in the first place? We all just love somebody correcting us, right?

When Orel Hershiser was in his first season as a pitcher for the Los Angeles Dodgers, he had great talent but had not been able to translate that into success on the field. Early in the 1984 season, he was struggling with his control. Finally, Dodgers manager Tommy Lasorda called the young pitcher into his office for a verbal confrontation that Hershiser later referred to as "The Sermon on the Mound."

Lasorda told Hershiser that he was capable of much better work than he was doing and that he owed it to the team to reach his potential. Hershiser took the rebuke to heart and approached the game with a new attitude. He went on to win the Cy Young award as baseball's best pitcher in 1988 while leading the Dodgers to the World Series title.[16]

What's the lesson here? If Hershiser had not reacted correctly to his manager's analysis, it is unlikely that he would ever have reached such victory. I think that's the point Paul is making here. Hey Ephesians, if you're not walking right, then let's start to because there's a game to win out there and you're called by God to do it.

But what is this "calling" that we've been "called" to in verse one? We're supposed to walk in a manner that is in balance to it, so what is it? There are three sides to our calling.[17]

It's a **Humble Calling**. 1 Corinthians 1:26, *"For consider your calling, brothers: not many of you were wise according to worldly standards, not many were powerful, not many were of noble birth."* There are two sides to a humble calling. First, don't let anyone look down upon you because they don't recognize what God's doing. Second, don't allow yourself to look too highly of yourself because God has recognized you for His purposes. There's this balancing act as a Christian, walk with confidence yet without pride. But how do I do that? Well, remember, Christ is our example.

It's a **Holy Calling**. 2 Timothy 1:9, *"who saved us and called us to a holy calling"* to be set apart for God's use. Think of the holy land, or the holy of holies, or the nation of Israel that was set aside for God's purposes. That purpose was holy. In the same way, your calling from God is to be set apart (*from the world*) for His purposes. It's a holy calling.

It's a **Heavenly Calling**. Philippians 3:14, Hebrews 3:1, *"I press on toward the goal for the prize of the upward call of God in Christ Jesus."* & *"Therefore, holy brothers, you who share in a heavenly calling."* We serve a King and His Kingdom. The kingdom of this world will falter and fail as the Kingdom of God continues. It's important for those who have been called by God to keep their focus upon a heavenly kingdom and not a temporal, ever-changing, earthly, or all too human reality.

We are like a prize fighter who enters the ring, like a runner who enters the race, or like a business person

Freedom

opening a new location, when we do so we do it to win. That's Paul's first point here. Stay dedicated to a Quest for Unity if you desire to achieve it. Nobody just finds unity. It doesn't just pop up on its own. We have to work for it, live for it, and protect it when we achieve it because it's a holy and heavenly thing. Paul then goes on in verse two, to share four evidences of unity.

The Qualities of Unity

"With all humility and gentleness, with patience, bearing with one another in love." Ephesians 4:2

Have you ever wondered what unity within a group of people would look like? Then look no further than to the actions found in this insightful verse. Paul describes four essentials to build and keep unity within the Body of Christ. Imagine four fortified corners of a beautiful picture. Without this proper support, the framework of unity would easily disassemble, and our picture of harmony would collapse upon itself in destruction. Let's take a look at these four important qualities.

Humility. Philippians 2:5-8, *"Have this mind among yourselves, which is yours in Christ Jesus, who, though he was in the form of God, did not count equality with God a thing to be grasped, but emptied himself, by taking the form of a servant, being born in the likeness of men. And being found in human form, he humbled himself by becoming obedient to the point of death, even death on a cross."*

There's a grand idea of preference within this text. It's

sort of like a story my wife told me many years ago when we were in college. Prior to us dating, she was seeing another guy. To my benefit, this dude made a colossal mistake one day. As they were getting into his car, she reached over from her passenger seat to change the radio station. I guess she didn't like his style of music. I can't imagine why! As she reached over, her then-boyfriend pulled her hand away and said, "Don't do that. This is my car and I'll be the one to change the station if I want to." Needless to say, that relationship didn't last very long. So, to my advantage, my now single *future wife* was back on the market. I swooped in, and the rest is history. What happened there?

It's simple, he didn't prefer her needs over his own. That's what Paul is getting at here when we prefer (or give preference to) what others want over what we want, that helps to build unity. When we refuse to give preference, relationships break apart. Paul gives us the ultimate example of learning preference found within the life of Christ. Simply put, Christ selected us over his own preferences. He laid down the independent use of his divine properties to connect with our human deficiencies. He took upon himself our penalty so that we could have liberty. So, Paul is saying if you want unity, it starts with this idea of giving preference to another person first.

Gentleness. Matthew 11:29, *"Take my yoke upon you, and learn from me, for I am gentle and lowly in heart, and you will find rest for your souls."*

"This word, *gentle*, is also translated *meek* and carries far greater meaning than a modern English understanding, i.e., being nice to others.

Bible commentator Larry Pierce writes, "Meekness toward God is that disposition of spirit in which we accept His dealings with us as good, and therefore without disputing or resisting. In the OT, the meek are those wholly relying on God rather than their own strength to defend against injustice. Thus, meekness toward evil people means knowing God is permitting the injuries they inflict, that He is using them to purify His elect, and that He will deliver His elect in His time. (Isa 41:17, Luke 18:1-8) Gentleness or meekness is the opposite of self-assertiveness and self-interest. It stems from trust in God's goodness and control over the situation. The gentle person is not occupied with self at all. This is a work of the Holy Spirit, not of the human will. "[18] (Gal 5:23.)

Patience. Hebrews 6:12, *"...imitators of those who through faith and patience inherit the promises."* There's an element of time with this idea of patience, right? Inheriting a promise takes time. Think of a family inheritance or your retirement portfolio. We have to wait to receive the benefit if we want the full value. The original language means, to have a long temper which by definition would be the opposite of a short temper. Paul is saying don't be quick to snap at each other, but rather have patience with each other if you want to have the full value and benefit of unity. So that's humility, gentleness, and patience. Let's look at the 4th quality.

Forbearance. 2 Thess 1:4, *"Therefore we ourselves boast about you in the churches of God for your steadfastness and faith in all your persecutions and in the afflictions that you are enduring."* This idea of forbearance is very robust. It means, "to hold oneself up against, i.e., figuratively put up with." Picture putting your back up against a wall about to fall over and your forbearance with that wall is keeping it standing. That's the idea here. We hold one another other up when we're about to fall. The second idea here is to "bear with, endure, or in some cases suffer with someone." When was the last time you suffered with another member of the Body of Christ? Paul says this is a sign of unity and a building block to even greater harmony.

So, we have the Quest for Unity and now the Qualities of Unity; let's take a look at the final aspect of Living in Unity as described by Paul in Ephesians 4:1-3. It's called the Quilt of Unity.

The Quilt of Unity

"Eager to maintain the unity of the Spirit in the bond of peace." Ephesians 4:3

In part two of Paul's letter, these last few words of his opening sentence conclude with a word picture of maintaining unity through a special bond between members. Paul then continues to explain the seven ways in which Christians are connected. Like a multifaceted quilt, the look and feel of the way we do ministry are connected by the special spiritual threads between us. Those threads are described for us in verses 4-6.

Freedom

But before we get there... what is unity? "Unity is not union ("being connected to one another"), uniformity ("being exactly like one another"), or unanimity ("always agreeing with one another"). It is an organic oneness based on Christ as the common center. Believers are required not to **create unity** but to **keep the unity** that already is theirs in Christ."[19]

Romans 12:5, *"So we, though many, are one body in Christ, and individually members one of another."*

We see this idea of teamwork. Imagine a football team of 11 guys running a play on offense. As every player does his part, *as designed*, the chance for a successful play to develop increases. And the more times they run successful plays, again and again and again, their chances to win the game continue to grow exponentially.

That's a similar thing Paul is saying here. Maintain your bond of peace so each of you can do your part, *as designed*, by the coach. Minimize your mistakes, reduce your penalties, and move the ball down the field. Stay focused on your part of the play. Use your gifts and do your job.

I would be careless in my duties if I neglected to point out Paul's mention for us to be *"eager to maintain the unity"* between us. I have to confess I haven't always been eager to do the right thing when it comes to some of those in the Body of Christ. I have been eager to dismiss some people, that's for sure. I know it's not right, but hey, let's be real.

Don't act like you've never been upset or mad at another believer. I've been around Christians long enough to know that we all tend to get on each other's nerves. When that happens, we are bent toward being willing to divide ourselves from each other instead of showing grace and seeking peace in a swift manner.

That's the point here, be eager to reconcile. Be swift to show mercy. Be quick to restore the bond of peace. Too many times, it seems to me, that we take our time to reconcile differences. Allow me to encourage you to rectify the situation faster next time you need to. And if you have yet to clear up any old differences, allow Paul's words to encourage you to make amends today. Seriously, start today.

Following verse 3, Paul continues to list seven truths that create this spiritual bond between Christians. Ephesians 4:4-6, *"There is one body and one Spirit—just as you were called to the one hope that belongs to your call— one Lord, one faith, one baptism, one God and Father of all, who is over all and through all and in all."*

One Body – The collection of all of God's people. Even though you may not always feel like you're connected, or that you want to get disconnected, The Bible is clear, we are all connected as one family.

One Spirit – The Holy Spirit indwells each of us. It amazes me every time I travel to a different culture and immediately, I feel at home with other Christians. That's the Holy Spirit in me and the Holy Spirit in them.

One Hope – The return of Christ one day for each of us.

We don't grieve or get worried about the future. We've read to the end of the story. We know how this movie ends. The Lord will return and that gives us hope.

One Lord – Jesus is our Savior and Lord. One day, the Scripture tells us, every knee will bow, and every tongue confess that Jesus Christ is Lord. It's not a matter of if you will confess it, it's a matter of when.

One Faith – Salvation by grace, through faith, in Christ. We place our trust in Christ and in nothing else. Christianity is not spelled DO but rather DONE. The work has been done by Christ there is nothing left for us to do.

One Baptism – All believers are baptized by the Holy Spirit into the Body of Christ at the moment of salvation. Water baptism, by immersion, follows as an outward sign of our inward commitment to Christ.

One Father – The heavenly Father, as described by Christ, has lavished his love upon us as his children. We are in right relationship with him through Christ and have available all rights and privileges as his children and joint heirs with Christ.

As we step back from this passage of scripture, we can almost see the quilted patchwork of the various ministries within the Body of Christ. And as we look closely, we can see seven golden threads woven between each of these ministries that create a beautiful mosaic of ministry platforms around the globe. Yet supernaturally, somehow, we are all connected through a shared unity. That unity is found in the oneness baked into these seven truths.

In *The Pursuit of God*, author A.W. Tozer summarized the whole concept of unity and how powerful it can be in the following way:

"Has it ever occurred to you that one hundred pianos all tuned to the same fork are automatically tuned to each other? They are of one accord by being tuned, not to each other, but to another standard to which each one must individually bow. So, one hundred worshipers [*meeting*] together, each one looking away to Christ, are in heart nearer to each other than they could possibly be, were they to become 'unity' conscious and turn their eyes away from God to strive for closer fellowship."[20]

As we turn our attention heavenward, to the worship of our Savior, it is Christ that will maintain our common unity found explicitly in him, by him, and for his glory.

Conclusion

So, we have the Quest, Qualities, and Quilt of unity all within the first three verses of Ephesians chapter four. Let me conclude with this.

A College football coach and his recent All-American linebacker were talking at the end of the season. As fate would have it, the linebacker's last season ended, and he didn't know what to do prior to starting his NFL career. The coach really liked his player and asked him to sit down for a moment as he had an idea.

Freedom

The coach said: "You know we're going to need some help recruiting a new class of guys in here for next year before you head off to the NFL next summer. I was hoping you could help me find some of the best guys out there to fill the roster."

The player said, "You bet coach, I'd love to help. What are you looking for?"

"Well," the coach said, "you know kind of players that when you knock 'em over they don't get up?"

"Yep," said the player. "Well, we don't want those types," said the coach.

"And you know the kind of players who you can knock over a few times and they get up, but after four of five real good hits, they don't get back up?"

"Yep," said the player, "I know that kind too, don't like 'em too much to be honest with you." "Well, we don't want those guys either," said the coach.

"And you know the kind of player that you can knock down again and again and again…and they get right back…." at this point, the linebacker moved to the front of his chair and stood up and said…

"YES! I know those guys; you want me to find 'em for you coach? That's something I can get excited about."

The coach looked at the player and said, "Nope… but what I do want, is the guy who's going around knocking everybody down." "Find that guy for me."

T.K. Anderson

It may be impressive to knock people over in football, but in our Christian faith, it's the complete opposite. Sometimes it's easier to illustrate a point by showing the reverse concept. Listen, instead of being a bruising linebacker within the Body of Christ, let's be the ones to show unity and keep the unity we have in Christ. Stay focused on your end of the deal and do the job God has set aside for you to do. The rest of the team is counting on you.

You may be thinking today that this is all great stuff if you've already stepped over the line and become a Christian. You may be saying to yourself, "I can see how and why you guys get all fired up about being together, supporting each other, and bailing each other out. But you don't know my life, I'm alone. I've burned the bridges and there's no coming back. I'm far from God."

"I'm the guy who's pushed away every possible person, organization, or entity designed to assist me. There's no hope for me. I'm cornered, isolated, and miserable. I don't know who I am anymore. I've fallen for everything because I haven't stood for anything. I don't know what to do!"

Well, can I share with you that you're the exact style of person that Jesus specializes in with his message of love, purpose, and promise of joy. Joy, you say? Yes, joy, true joy! You can have it as you put your trust in Christ right now. Don't wait! Don't delay! Quit putting off until tomorrow what you can take care of today.

There's a wonderful story in the Bible found in the fourth chapter of the Gospel of John. In this story Jesus strikes up

Freedom

a conversation with a woman who is struggling with her personal identity and low social standing because of a series of poor life choices. She's broken, full of remorse, and a spiritual mess.

Can you relate? What starts as a casual noon-time conversation around a Samaritan well (*AKA the town water cooler*) ends up as a dialogue that is transformative for not only her but her whole town as well.

In a nutshell, Jesus confronts her poor life choices, and she readily concedes, but then, in a moment of life change, she realizes that he's offering her a chance to leave that all behind and begin a new life as a child of God. Jesus tells her,

> *"Everyone who drinks of this water will be thirsty again,[14] but whoever drinks of the water that I will give him will never be thirsty again. The water that I will give him will become in him a spring of water welling up to eternal life." [15] The woman said to him, 'Sir, give me this water so that I will not be thirsty or have to come here to draw water.'"*[21] John 4:13-15

The Bible goes on to explain that she received the message of salvation from Jesus and promptly went back into town to tell all her neighbors, friends, and anyone who would listen, about the forgiveness of Christ and that Jesus is the Savior of the world. The townspeople came out to see for themselves and they invited Jesus to stay with them to learn more. He did so, for two days. They were so amazed by his presence that the Bible says, *"Many Samaritans from that town believed in him because of the woman's testimony."* [22] (John 4:39)

Their lives were changed in an instant because this one woman had enough courage to take Jesus at his word. Do you have enough courage to do that today? Trust me, he won't let you down. God hasn't given up on you, so don't give up on yourself. Come to him today and let him direct your life so you can begin to experience true joy and can be a blessing to those around you.

Chapter Three

Live in Power

Ephesians 6:10-18

In the late 1800's Thomas Edison changed our world with the invention of the light bulb. But, more importantly, he powered these bulbs with a new electric producing generator. We see and experience this two-part invention every day.

The first public event for Edison's new invention took place on September 4th, 1882. The New York Times recorded the occasion by writing, "At 3:00 p.m., New York City was illuminated with the flip of a switch, electric lights brightened our city for the first time. It happened at Pearl Street Station, the first central power station in the world. Operated by Thomas A. Edison and his Edison Electric Illuminating Company of New York."[23] One hundred and thirty-six years ago, with the flip of a switch, our world was changed.

In a similar way, immediately coinciding with salvation, the Bible promises us our lives will be changed. With the flip of a switch, God illuminates the hearts and souls of mankind. But if we have access to a power source greater than Edison's generators why do so many Christians lack the necessary power to overcome the difficult circumstances of life?

Power, it's a powerful word, isn't it? Depending on who controls it and how they utilize it determines immensely different outcomes both for the user and in many cases the wounded. But it doesn't have to be this way. Power is like fire; it all depends on how you use it. Power can be used for constructive purposes, and it can be used for destructive purposes.

When understood properly, harnessed appropriately, and utilized as designed, power is an amazing resource God has given us to overcome life's most challenging situations. How do I get it and how can I use it properly for God's glory?

You may be facing a tough situation today. Your problems may be big. They may be unsolvable. They may be exhausting or unbeatable, but don't give up hope just yet. You may be surprised to know you have a power source that is far bigger than any scenario you may be confronting.

Did you know you have a type of power that everyone in the world is craving? It's a power that can withstand any scenario. It's a power that goes deeper than any ocean, higher than any skyscraper, wider than any continent, and is stronger than any substance known to mankind. It's harder than diamonds, more valuable than gold, and more precious than silver. The best part, it's available to those who know Christ as their personal Savior.

In Ephesians chapter six, Paul continues in his letter to believers in Ephesus explaining how to live out the Christian life with real power. He explains to the new Christians there is a power flow, or current, in this present age that moves in the opposite direction from God. As we move against that current, in following Christ, it will be a battle. So, don't be surprised by the fight, Paul writes. Don't get caught up in the struggles and circumstances of life.

Remember, Paul calls out to his readers, in this battle God has not left us powerless, defenseless, or without a strategy. On the contrary, in Christ we have everything we need. Other disciples understood this power as well. Late in life, the Apostle Peter commented on this same issue. 2 Peter 1:3 captures his thought perfectly, *"His divine power has granted to us all things that pertain to life and godliness."*

Peter, Paul, and the early church leaders understood this principle. Paul just so happened to illustrate it for us in Ephesians chapter six using the picture of a Roman soldier.

One writer notes, "When we 'put on' Jesus Christ, we are protected by the only person Satan has never defeated. Using the armor of a Roman soldier as a model, the Apostle Paul describes how the Christian can stand strong in the midst of this ever-present, but unseen, spiritual battle."[24]

As Paul continued his writings from his house arrest in Rome, he was certain to point out that life isn't just about outward appearances but rather there is so much more happening within the realms we cannot see. And by actors we cannot perceive. Paul calls these invisible actors, *"the cosmic powers over this present darkness"* and *"spiritual forces of evil in the heavenly places."* (Ephesians 6:12) To Paul, what we see with our physical eyes is only a part of the whole picture.

It's like us watching a TV screen, we can't see the three dimensions in the picture, let alone how the digital or analog signal is sent or received by our TV. There is more to the story if we want the complete picture. It's the same way in our personal lives. There is so much more happening behind the scenes.

T.K. Anderson

I want you to gain better control by looking behind the scenes with me today. Let's find out how we can live in a way that allows us to shrug off the bad circumstances as Paul did. And answer the question, how can we access a kind of power to live above life's circumstances and not just live through them?

We can do that first by recognizing our source of power.

Recognize Our Source of Power

"[10]*Finally, be strong in the Lord and in the strength of his might….*[18]*praying at all times in the Spirit, with all prayer and supplication."* Ephesians 6:10,18

Paul starts the last section of his letter with the word, *'finally.'* As he writes his last portion describing this epic and unseen spiritual battle, he writes in light of all that he has just communicated. It's a reminder to his readers to go back and recall all of God's provisions for us regarding how we are to walk out this earthly life. Especially in light of the conflicts and struggles we face in this present fight.

Pastor and author David Guzik explains, "Paul is essentially saying, in light of all that God has done for you. In light of the glorious standing, you have as a child of God. In light of His great plan of the ages that God has made you part of. In light of the plan for Christian maturity and growth, He gives to you. In light of the conduct God calls every believer to live. In light of the filling of the Spirit and our walk in the Spirit. In light of all this, there is a battle to fight in the Christian life."[25]

The first step to recognizing our source of power is to recognize the Person of Power. In this *power passage,* Ephesians 6:10-18, Paul bookends for us two important principles regarding our source of power and how to access it. Notice in verse ten he writes, *"Be strong in the Lord and in the strength of his might."* This is a clear reference to the Person of our Power and his ability to empower us, and in case you're wondering, that person happens to be Christ.

The thought here is to *"put on'"* Christ before we *"put on'"* the spiritual armor he's about to describe. If we try to put on the armor without the power and strength of Christ within us, our weakness will be exposed, and we'll simply stumble and fall within the first moments of the first skirmish. It'll be over rather quickly. Sadly, this happens to way too many Christians. The lesson here is when we attempt to operate in our own strength we will fail.

Paul doesn't want his disciples to falter, so from his prison accommodations in Rome, he writes up an amazing pep talk that rivals the best halftime speech from the greatest of coaches. This phrase, *"be strong in Lord and the strength of his might"*, most likely came from a passage in 1 Samuel 30:6, *"And David was greatly distressed, for the people spoke of stoning him, because all the people were bitter in soul, each for his sons and daughters. But David strengthened himself in the LORD his God."*

The Bible speaks of us strengthening ourselves in the Lord, but what does that mean? This is a reference to the spiritual discipline of worship. David, when he was distressed, down, or disappointed would call out to God through song. We have the lyrics to many of those songs in the book of Psalms. As you may know, the book of Psalms is actually a collection of poems put to song.

Here's a good working definition, "The word psalm comes from the Greek word which means *"to pluck."* That word gave rise to psalmos, which means "a song sung to harp music." Finally, the English word psalm means "*song.*" The book of Psalms is a book of songs that is sometimes called "Israel's National Hymnbook." The title of the book in Hebrew is *Tehillim*, which means "Praises."[26]

There's a second reason we know Paul was speaking about employing the power of song to strengthen ourselves in the Lord. He just covered the idea in Chapter five. Look at what he wrote in Ephesians 5:18-20, *"[18]And do not get drunk with wine, for that is debauchery, but be filled with the Spirit, [19]addressing one another in psalms and hymns and spiritual songs, singing and making melody to the Lord with your heart, [20]giving thanks always and for everything to God the Father in the name of our Lord Jesus Christ."*

One of the ways in which we are filled with the Spirit is through music and song. Don't ever underestimate the power of music and song. It's a means by which we are ushered into the presence of God, or conversely, when utilized not within its intended purpose, can actually pull us away from the Lord. So, be strengthened in the Lord, and you can do that through worship, Paul says. Then he continues with a second bookend in chapter 6, *"[18] Praying at all times in the Spirit, with all prayer and supplication."*

The second step in recognizing our source of power is remembering the Power of Prayer. But what is prayer?

Prayer is the simple act of asking God for his will to be done. It's not mystical, magical, or mysterious. But yet, do we take full advantage of our open line of communication with our Creator? Sadly, if we're brutally honest, most of us don't. However, when we don't pray, we miss out on many of the things in life God wants to bless us with, protect us from, or just plain amaze us with.

While crossing the Atlantic on an ocean liner, a famous pastor was asked to address a group of passengers. At the captain's request, he spoke on "Answered Prayer." An agnostic who was present at the service was asked by his friends, "What did you think of the pastor's sermon?" He answered, "I didn't believe a word of it." That afternoon the pastor went to speak to a second group of passengers. Many of the earlier listeners went along, including the agnostic. Before heading to the service, the agnostic put two oranges in his pocket.

On his way, he passed an elderly woman sitting in her deck chair fast asleep. Her hands were open. In the spirit of fun, the agnostic put the two oranges in her outstretched palms. After the meeting, he saw the old lady happily eating one of the pieces of fruit. "You seem to be enjoying that orange," he remarked with a smile. "Yes, sir," she replied, "My Father is very good to me." "Your father? Surely your father can't be still alive!" "Praise God," she replied, "He is very much alive." "What do you mean?" pressed the agnostic. She explained, "I'll tell you, sir. I have been seasick for days. I was asking God somehow to send me an orange. I suppose I fell asleep while I was praying. When I awoke, I found He had not only sent me one orange but two!"[27]

Why do we employ prayer as a last resort rather than first line of defense? If life on this earth really is a battle (*as described by Paul in Ephesians 6*) then we should use the most effective strategies first. We tend to entangle ourselves with all the details and issues of this life. Yet the Bible encourages us to do the exact opposite.

Paul wrote this to a young protégé named Timothy. In one of his personal letters he wrote, *"No one serving as a soldier entangles himself in the affairs of this life, that he might please the one having enlisted him."* (2 Timothy 2:4) You've been enlisted by God. Stay focused on him and his plan.

Prayer is a spiritual discipline that helps us connect to God and in essence disentangle us from the affairs of this life. If you want a tool to help you become more Christ-centered, rather than circumstance-centered, then start with prayer. When we look heavenward, the concerns of this world fade away. There's an old song we used to sing called, *Turn Your Eyes Upon Jesus,* written in 1922 by Helen Lemmel. Her words capture this idea perfectly:

Turn your eyes upon Jesus
Look full in His wonderful face
And the things of Earth will grow strangely dim
In the light of His glory and grace[28]

Some people ask me, "How do I start to pray?" One of the best ways is to start singing. If you're like me, as you sing through this tune in your head it's as if your spirit is automatically lifted toward heaven. The burdens of my heart roll away. We can sense the presence of God strengthening our spirit as we express our concerns in prayer.

Once we've been strengthened in the Lord and spent time in prayer making our requests made known to God, we're ready for the second aspect of learning how to overcome life's circumstances. That's to resolve to go against the current.

Freedom

Resolve to go Against the Current

"¹¹Put on the whole armor of God, that you may be able to stand against the schemes of the devil. ¹²For we do not wrestle against flesh and blood, but against the rulers, against the authorities, against the cosmic powers over this present darkness, against the spiritual forces of evil in the heavenly places." (Ephesians 6:11-12)

In this next section of Paul's writing, we find a two-part explanation of this unseen battle we're a part of. Starting in verse 11 we see a Plot to Sweep Us Downstream. If you have ever spent time fishing or boating, especially on a large river, you're familiar with the concept of a current and the tremendous amount of pull or force it contains.

That's the idea Paul is getting at here. Except he's not talking about a physical current directing a boat downstream, rather he's indicating our entire world is drifting downstream away from God and we will get caught up in its pull if we don't do something proactive about it. His encouragement is for believers to stand against the current, and as we stand, stand firm. The word, *"against,"* is used six times in these two verses. This is a strong indication that we are to resist the dark forces flowing against us.

Paul uses a wonderfully descriptive set of words in these two sentences so that we can clearly understand what this battle is all about. He uses the phrase, his'-tay-mee – pross [hístēmi - prós] which means to *"stand against,"* as in "stand against the schemes of the devil." It carries this idea of being immovable as you face toward something. In other words, our enemy, Satan is making plans for our destruction. So, don't get caught up in that current (the direction of that flow) but rather resolve to stand strong in the Lord and against this current as you face upstream (or face against it).

Paul continues with another word, pal'-ay [pálē], which means 'to wrestle.' Paul explains that *"we do not wrestle against flesh and blood,"* but rather against dark forces attempting to "throw us" off course. This word, *"wrestle",* means exactly that. It's the same word we use today which means *"to throw."*

In the sport of wrestling, we throw somebody in such a way as to gain victory over them. So, this two-part picture is one in which we are to stand strong, stubbornly facing upstream as we wrestle (or throw) our enemy into surrender. We do this because if we don't, we will find ourselves thrown under the current of our culture through the deceptive and crafty schemes of our enemy.

In late September 1864, Confederate General Nathan Bedford Forrest was leading his troops north from Decatur, Alabama, toward Nashville. But to make it to Nashville, Forrest would have to defeat the Union army at Athens, Alabama. When the Union commander, Colonel Wallace Campbell, refused to surrender, Forrest asked for a personal meeting and took Campbell on an inspection of his troops. But each time they left a detachment, the Confederate soldiers simply packed up and moved to another position, artillery and all. Forrest and Campbell would then arrive at the new encampment and continue to tally up the impressive number of Confederate soldiers and weaponry. By the time they returned to the fort, Campbell was convinced he couldn't win and surrendered unconditionally![29]

Freedom

Satan likes to mislead us too. He wants us to think we can't stand against his formidable current. If we get to that point and voluntarily surrender, we are essentially repeating the same mistake as the deceived General. Don't be deceived, *"He who is in you is greater than he who is in the world."* (1 John 4:4)

So how do I anchor down my life in such a way as to not be carried away by the current of our culture, double-crossed by the deceptions of the deceiver, or circumvented by the circumstance of life? That's the second part of this set of verses. We can create anchors in our life as we Remain Persistent in Our Convictions. Famed World War II tank commander General George Patton said, "Courage is fear holding on a minute longer."[30]

Do you remember the story of Daniel and the Lion's Den? It's detailed for us in Chapter six of the book that bears his name. Do you recall what brought him to this perilous place? It was his resolve to not go along with the current of his culture. The political leaders of Daniel's day created a set of rules that if violated would put him in a den of lions. Daniel refused to be carried along by this deceptive decision. He ended up in a precarious situation in which God was ultimately honored by delivering his servant from the plans of his enemy.

Yet, to properly understand how Daniel could stand against the wicked scheme of his enemies, you have to go back to the beginning of his story. Five chapters earlier, in Daniel 1:8, the Bible captures the beginning of his story this way, *"But Daniel resolved not to defile himself with the royal food and wine."* (NIV) Other translations use the phrases, *"purposed in his heart,"* *"determined not to,"* or *"made up his mind not to"* go against God's plan for his life. In essence, he was resolved to stand firm against the current at any cost. It was a decision of his mind made in advance.

When the Babylonians captured the people of Israel and brought them back to Babylon, they hand-picked the best and brightest of the people of God to serve in a quasi-leadership role. They hoped to convert the young Jewish leaders into examples for other captures to follow. Yet, the Bible details for us Daniel's decision to rise above their plan and instead pursue God's plan for his life.

Daniel's life is an example for us in that we too can purpose in our hearts and resolve to not give into the plans of this world. We can instead *"put on the whole armor of God"* as encouraged in verse 11. This verb Paul uses here for 'put on', is in the sense of sinking into a garment, like the putting on of a robe. So, if you want to be resolved to go against the current and stand firm in your convictions for Christ, you can anchor yourself in by putting on the armor of God. This brings us to the third aspect of learning how we can overcome life's circumstances, and that's by remembering to utilize our cache of weapons.

Remember Our Cache of Weapons

"[11]Put on the whole armor of God... [13]Therefore, take up the whole armor of God... [14]Stand therefore, having fastened on the belt of truth, and having put on the breastplate of righteousness, [15]and, as shoes for your feet, having put on the readiness given by the gospel of peace. [16]In all circumstances take up the shield of faith, with which you can extinguish all the flaming darts of the evil

one; ¹⁷and take the helmet of salvation and the sword of the Spirit which is the word of God." Ephesians 6:11,13-17

Much of the Christian experience is a defensive experience according to Paul's description here. The reason for this is we live in a fallen world that is prone to sin. Sin, simply meaning actions and attitudes designed to set itself up against the things of God or the will of God. So, when we come to Christ and want to live for Christ and do things the way he wants us to, there's going to be this constant battle.

In other words, if you're not a Christian then there's no battle to fight. You're simply going with the flow as everyone else. But for those who God has called out from this world, there will be a battle. The phrase *"put on," "fasten on,"* or *"take up"* is used seven times in these six verses. Paul is saying, we need to buckle up and be ready to fight.

Remember, Paul was writing from Rome while under house arrest. He was guarded 24/7 by Roman soldiers. We shouldn't be surprised that he used this metaphor of armor to make his point to the Ephesians. As a follower of Jesus Christ, God wants you to know he hasn't left you defenseless. You have a stockpile of weapons available to you in the battle.

Imagine for a moment you've been transported back in time to a medieval battlefield. You look across the field and see a formidable army waiting to attack. Then you realize you're not alone, as you survey the surroundings and notice others dressed as you are, wearing the same colors and carrying the same insignia. A commander approaches and says, *"Hurry up and get your armor on, the enemy is about to attack."* He points in the direction of a group of wagons filled with weaponry for you and your fellow soldiers.

That's the picture Paul is painting here. We are in the middle of a battlefield and our King has not left us empty-handed. How foolish would it be to not fit ourselves for battle with the weaponry he's provided? Yet, how many Christians go into battle without their armor, or simply do not heed the directives of their spiritual commanders?

Nonetheless, because you want to win this battle and bring honor to your King, you approach the stockpile of weapons with the desire to be prepared. As you wait in line, you notice the expressions on each soldier's face dramatically change once they receive their instructions before their return to the battlefield.

"They are now properly equipped," you hear a commander pronounce boldly. What once was a face of fear and intimidation has changed to a gaze of assured victory. You can't help but wonder, is this what Paul's countenance was when he wrote out this striking description in Ephesians chapter six? *"I think, perhaps it was,"* you conclude.

"It's your turn now," you overhear an unknown voice. It's the quartermaster from the top of a loaded wagon. He's an old and wiser soldier, who's blazed fiercely across many battlefields. He leans over and kindly hands you a few key provisions. *"So, what are these formidable weapons of spiritual warfare?"* You ask. *"Allow me to explain,"* says the seasoned warrior.

"This first item is a **belt of truth**. *Use this to counter your enemy who is the father of lies. (John 8:4) Our King is the way, the truth,*

and the life. (John 14:6) In him is life eternal and all truth is found in him." As you gather up your garments and tighten the belt, he looks you squarely in the eye and says, *"Truth is not a concept or a precept, truth is a person. Always remember that fact, as a battlefield by design, is intended to deceive you. Let the Truth be your guide."*

He reaches back and hands you a slightly larger, more substantial piece of armor. *"This next item is the **breastplate of righteousness**. Use this to protect yourself from your enemy who wants nothing more than to pierce your heart. If you rely on your own righteousness, you'll no more be protecting yourself than with a muddy garment or autumn leaf. (Isaiah 64:6) You'll be easy to corrupt and will soon be swept away by the first sudden breeze."*

As you lower it over your shoulders, you notice an inscription engraved on the inside, *"Righteousness is given through faith in Jesus Christ to all who believe."* (Romans 3:22)

"Now hurry, take these shoes," he says. *"They are **shoes of the gospel of peace** and use them to secure your footing as you war. The enemy desires for you to be trapped in a root of bitterness and hatred toward others." (Hebrews 12:15.)* As you lace up your shoes, he lowers his voice and quietly explains, *"Remember the cross and that it's through Christ that we have peace with God. Take peace and move swiftly through the hatred of this world. Seek to bring reconciliation, not resentment." (*2 Corinthians 5:18)

"Here is your protection from the enemy's lethal arrows," the quartermaster says as he hands you a strikingly fashioned rectangular and bowl-shaped shield. He undeniably continues, *"Your chief enemy is famous for shooting fiery arrows attempting*

to pierce your divine armor and scorch your eternal soul." As you promptly begin to look over this newest piece of equipment, the quartermaster resumes, *"The arrows of fear and doubt, which are counterclaims of faith, will be doused as you remember the One in whom your faith rests."*

"Lastly," he proclaims, *"your **shield of faith** is strategically designed to work together with others on the frontline. Don't be afraid to link up with those around you. The combined strength of your shields can withstand any attack from the front, top, and either side."* (1 Thessalonians 3:2)

"Hold on, one moment," he says. He briefly scrambles around to the back side of the wagon gathering two additional pieces of equipment. *"Here, put this helmet on. It is the **helmet of salvation**."* As you slip it on, he continues, *"This will guard the battle for your mind, as the enemy attacks your thinking remember to hold every thought captive to the mind of Christ."* (2 Corinthians 10:5)

As he speaks, you recall the words of Peter's second letter, *"For we did not follow cleverly devised myths when we made known to you the power and coming of our Lord Jesus Christ, but we were eyewitnesses of his majesty"* 2 Peter 1:16. At that moment, you're reminded that salvation doesn't dwell in a fairytale, but is engrained in history. God came to earth, became one of us, walked among us, was crucified for us, yet rose again to redeem us, seal us, and call us to serve him and him alone.

"Finally," he calls out, *"you may have noticed the previous five weapons are designed for defensive purposes. Yet, this last weapon is for offense."* He then hands you a beautifully crafted

Freedom

blade looking as if it were forged from the fires of the sun. Etched within its handle are the words, **Sword of the Spirit**. Its brilliant shine radiates the brightness around it as if to magnify the light while simultaneously dissipating the darkness. *"It's your sword,"* he says, *"It's been specially crafted by the Word of God to slay your enemy. This sword is your ultimate weapon to defeat your foe, against this weapon he has no defense."*

You stand back, carefully survey the complex field and review your options. As you do so, you can't help but instantly notice every extraordinary piece of armor is intentionally designed for you to be forward-facing. If you were to ever turn and run away from the battle that's when you'd be most vulnerable. As the light goes on with this new reality, the timeworn quartermaster approaches you and cleverly asks, *"I see you made the connection with how our King designed your armor to be used?"*

He smiles gratefully and continues thoughtfully, *"Fight well for my specified time is almost done. I have a feeling the King will be calling me home soon. I have fought the good fight; I have successfully run the race"* 2 Timothy 4:7. *We dearly need you to fight well, and at some point, the King will properly call you to take my place. For we have a host of recruits coming to the front lines every day. We'll need skillful warriors like you to powerfully aid in training up the next generation. And one glorious day, when He gives the word, you too will join me in the King's Palace. I hear there's quite a reunion arranged for us there." (*Revelation 19:6-9 and John 14:1-4)

That may not be exactly what Paul was trying to get across in this passage, but it may have been something like that. He wants you and me to know that we are not alone in this battle and when life's circumstances get to a point where we feel overwhelmed, we should remember we have a cache of spiritual weapons.

Conclusion

We started this message with the question: "Why do so many Christians lack the necessary power to overcome the difficult circumstances of life?" What we discovered is based upon Paul's writings to the Ephesians. Christians don't actually lack basic power, but rather they are not utilizing the needed power that's available.

We first have to recognize our source of power, who is Christ. We are encouraged to *"put on"* Christ before we *"put on"* the spiritual armor available to us. One of the ways we can *"put on"* Christ is through the spiritual disciplines of worship and prayer. As we turn our eyes upon Jesus, the things of earth grow strangely dim, in the light of his glory and grace.

Rightly comparing our problems to the incompressible nature of our God helps us to rightly conclude our circumstances. Have you recognized Christ as your source of power?

Secondly, we need to resolve ourselves to go against the current. We discovered there is a plot to sweep us downstream and to throw us under the current so that we are crushed. But as we remain persistent in our convictions for Christ, we will in essence be "standing against" the schemes of our enemy.

As the prophet Daniel purposed in his heart not to be influenced by his culture, we too can purpose in our hearts to go against the plans of our adversary. Have you purposed in your heart to stand

Freedom

against the schemes of your adversary?

Lastly, we are encouraged to utilize all six weapons provided to us in our cache of spiritual armor. We have access to five defensive weapons and one offensive weapon. Truth, righteousness, peace, faith, salvation, and the Word of God are all available to us and provided for us through Christ. Are you accessing the full complement of spiritual weapons available to you as you "put on" the full armor of Christ?

Yet even though we know these things to be true, some of us still struggle to put it all together. We feel as though our foundations are weak, our core is hollowed out, and we have few branches of life upon which to cling. What are we to do in this situation? Sometimes it feels like our life is about to fall over like the toppling of a huge redwood, for some it already has.

"At two o'clock on a Sunday afternoon, January 8, 2017, a giant fell to the earth, causing the ground to tremble like a palsied hand. One of the best-known giant sequoias, the Pioneer Cabin Tree, collapsed amid California storms. Pioneer Cabin, so named because its hollowed interior, was big enough for a home, had pointed upward for a thousand years. She was majestic to behold. But her core was gone, her limbs were brittle, her roots were shallow, and only a few branches still clung to life. When lashed by wind and water, the big tree tottered and tumbled and shattered on impact. Her millennium was over. Many of us are also teetering and tottering, never knowing when the next storm will come."[31]

Does that story relate to your life today? If you feel as though you're one storm away from destruction or you're already lying on the floor of the forest splintered, cracked, and broken, it doesn't have to stay that way. You have the power to choose a better life.

Can I encourage you today to make Christ the center of your life? Make Christ the core of your being and he will provide the strength you need to rise again from the ashes of defeat. His plan is to help you, heal you, restore you, remake you, all put together in one word… his plan is to love you into the person he's created you to be. If you haven't already, will you surrender your life to him? Can I encourage you to start the amazing journey he has marked out for your life?

"But you don't know what I've done," you might say. I've really messed up. I'm a long way away from God and I don't know how to get back. Listen, friend, it doesn't matter what you've done, Christ paid for that on the cross. That's the whole point of his suffering. He suffered so you wouldn't have to. When he forgives you, it's forever! And he does so because of his love for you.

The Bible couldn't be clearer when it says, *"As far as the east is from the west, so far does he remove our transgressions from us."* (Psalm 103:12) Or in Isaiah 1:18, *"Though your sins are like scarlet, they shall be as white as snow."*

R.A. Torrey, who served as the founding pastor of the Church of the Open Door in Los Angeles while also being well known as a foundational leader for both Moody Bible Institute and Biola University, summarized this entire point when he wrote,

"I look at the cross of Christ, and I know that atonement has been made for my sins. There no longer remains a single sin on me, no matter how many or how great my sins may have been. When Jesus died, He died as my representative, and I died in Him;

when He arose, He rose as my representative, and I arose in Him; when He ascended up on high and took His place at the right hand of the Father in the glory, He ascended as my representative and I ascended in Him, and today I am seated in Christ with God in the heavenlies."[32]

Are you seated with Christ? If you've accepted him into your heart as your Lord and Savior, then you are. You're free to live in Christ, enjoy living!

T.K. Anderson

Interlude between Ephesians and Philippians

As he rolled up the newly completed scroll, perhaps Paul reflected on his words to the Ephesians. "I've covered some weighty doctrine in this last letter," his thoughts continue, "I pray these words are a benefit to those who are fighting the deep intellectual and thorny philosophical battles in Ephesus. I'm optimistic these words will help to aid them in living out their faith in a way that honors our Lord. Under the direction of the Holy Spirit, I know this letter will be of tremendous use. Thank you, Lord, for the inspiration of this text." Now, we don't know for certain if this is what Paul was thinking, but we do know he most certainly kept these young Christians in his daily prayers and longed to be an encouragement to this inexperienced and early foundational congregation.

As Paul continued his day-to-day tasks under house arrest in Rome, we are most certain that visitors were a welcome respite from the potential monotony of confined quarters. Sometime during his prison sentence, with Timothy by his side, a friend named Epaphroditus made his way to Rome bringing necessary companionship and additional supplies to Paul. (Phil 4:18)

Epaphroditus arrived from another of Paul's newly established congregations, this time in the city of Philippi. It was during Paul's second great missionary journey that the church in Philippi was established, 10-plus years earlier, between the years A.D. 49-50.

Paul was originally prompted to go to Philippi by a vision of a man begging him to bring the gospel to Macedonia. We read about this famous journey in Acts chapter 16.

At the arrival of Epaphroditus, Paul was thrilled to hear the news regarding the followers of Christ from this important location. Philippi was an essential city in the province of Macedonia. It was located on the famous Via Egnatia, a leading thoroughfare, which connected the eastern provinces of the Roman empire to the city of Rome. Unfortunately, during his stay with Paul, Epaphroditus fell ill and came close to death. Nevertheless, he eventually recovered and was able to complete his service to Paul. (Phil. 2:27-30)

This sickness troubled Paul because he loved the believers in Philippi and held a special bond with many of them. Among them was Lydia, his hostess and founding member of the church in this city (Acts 16:14,40). Along with the jailor, whose entire household was saved, soon after he witnessed the power of praise as Paul and Silas were freed by a divine earthquake in the middle of the night. (Acts 16:25-34) And I'm sure special time was dedicated to hearing an update regarding the slave girl who was rescued from demonic powers during Paul's brief time of ministry in Philippi. (Acts 16:16-18)

For Paul, doing ministry in a city wasn't a one-time thing. It was about connection, both immediate and long-term. He maintained contact, revisited former locations, and ministered through correspondence and the sharing of offerings. So, hearing from visitors like Epaphroditus was medicine to his soul. He loved to hear about the expansion of God's Kingdom taking place in these various locations within the heart of the Roman empire. The

Freedom

Kingdom of God was advancing as the gates of hell were being overwhelmed as promised by Jesus. (Matthew 16:18) These were exciting days to be an apostle. Being on the front lines of God's new covenant with mankind was the place to be for Paul.

As Paul, Timothy and Epaphroditus shared stories, read scripture, shared their faith, and otherwise ministered to each other, at some point Paul must have felt it necessary to compose a letter. A letter intended for his dear friends in Philippi. A letter that Epaphroditus would hand deliver on his behalf. (Phil 2:25) The believers in Philippi faced three issues: First, there was persecution from the outside world. Second, false teachers were interfering with the church, as in other cities. And third, there was an unresolved conflict within the church between at least two of its members.

Within these conflicts, pressures, and problems Paul writes to give hope and a reminder to the Philippians of the great rejoicing we have in Christ. No matter the circumstances we know that true joy and genuine peace come from God and are found in Christ and Christ alone. A good summary of Paul's letter can be found in a comparison of the two different ways to live out our Christian life. Are you a 1:21 or 2:21 kind of Christian?

- Christ-centered Christian - *"For to me to live is Christ, and to die is gain."* (1:21)
- Self-centered Christian - *"For they all seek their own interests, not those of Jesus Christ."* (2:21)

Paul teaches that true rejoicing is found in living as a 1:21 Christian. Throughout the remainder of the letter, he tackles three main areas in the life of a believer. In doing so, he answers a considerable question. How can we best rejoice through hardship and humility as we embrace our heavenly citizenship? He insists within the epistle, that ultimately, we are free to rejoice in Christ.

Chapter Four

Rejoice in Hardship

Philippians 1:12-26

There's a very interesting principle found in the Bible that I'd like to share with you. Nestled far into the Book of Job we read a head-scratching truth, *"Hard times and trouble are God's way of getting our attention!"* Job 36:15. That statement sounds odd, doesn't it? We don't always understand it when it's happening to us, but we do know there's a whole lot to learn about this subject. If you're like me, sometimes it's the very problems we're experiencing that bring us closer to God. And other times it seems like hardships keep us from overcoming our disappointments and fears. Well, if there ever was a guy who knew about going through tough times, it most certainly was Job. But Job wasn't the only Biblical character to experience this truth. In that light, I'm excited to share with you what I've discovered in chapter one of Paul's letter to the people of Philippi.

One thing is for certain, Paul was a person who endured tremendous hardships. And thankfully, he wasn't shy about sharing his lessons on how to overcome those hardships with us. But, before we dive into Paul's letter to the Philippians, I want to share with you a different kind of letter. This message is a bit lighthearted and is from an unlucky man who definitely understood the meaning of having a tough day at the office.

T.K. Anderson

Here's a copy of his memo entitled, "*A Brick Layer's Insurance Claim.*"

Dear Sirs,

I am writing in response to your request for additional information. In block number three of the accident reporting form, I put "poor planning" as the cause of my accident. You said in your letter that I should explain more, and I trust that the following details are sufficient:

I am a bricklayer by trade. On the day of the accident, I was working alone on the roof of a new six-story building. When I completed my work, I discovered that I had about 500 pounds of bricks left over. Rather than carry the bricks down by hand I decided to lower them in a barrel by using a pulley, which fortunately was attached to the side of the building on the sixth floor.

Securing the rope at the ground level, I went up to the roof, swung the barrel out, and loaded the bricks into it. Then I went back to the ground and untied the rope, holding it tightly to insure a slow descent of the 500 pounds of bricks. You will note in block number 11 of the accident reporting form that I weigh 155 pounds.

Due to my surprise at being jerked off the ground so suddenly, I lost my presence of mind and forgot to let go of the rope. Needless to say, I proceeded at a rather rapid rate up the side of the building. In the vicinity of the third floor, I met the barrel coming down. This explains the fractured skull and broken collarbone.

Freedom

Slowed only slightly, I continued my rapid ascent, not stopping until the fingers of my right hand were two knuckles deep into the pulley. Fortunately, by this time I had regained my presence of mind and was able to hold tightly to the rope in spite of my pain. At approximately the same time, however, the barrel of bricks hit the ground - and the bottom fell out of the barrel. Devoid of the weight of the bricks, the barrel now weighed approximately 50 pounds.

I refer you again to my weight in block number 11. As you might imagine, I began a rapid descent down the side of the building. In the vicinity of the third floor, I met the barrel coming up. This accounts for the two fractured ankles and lacerations of my legs and lower body.

The encounter with the barrel, slowed me enough to lessen my injuries when I fell onto the pile of bricks, and fortunately, only three vertebrae were cracked. I am sorry to report, however, that as I lay there on the bricks in pain, unable to move, and watching the barrel six stories above - I again lost my presence of mind...I let go of the rope![33]

I don't know if that story is true, but I sure hope not. I wouldn't wish that kind of day on my worst enemy. But the fact remains, there are many days and seasons in life in which we feel like the bricklayer in this story. We're constantly getting battered, bruised, and hurt coming or going, all the while we're just looking for an efficient and hassle-free way to get through life.

If you're facing trouble, don't lose faith. The Lord is faithful and leaves us with this promise: *At the proper time we will reap a harvest if we do not give up." (Galatians 6:9)* Don't let go of the rope!

Paul understood the benefit of hardships, though. In fact, in 2 Corinthians 11:23-27, he detailed an unbelievable series of events he endured for the cause of Christ. He pointed to imprisonments, beatings, lashes, stonings, shipwrecks, dangers, hunger, thirst, anxiety, and more. Through all these trials and tribulations, however, Paul is steadfast in his belief that through these weaknesses he is made strong. In other words, the outward may be crushed, tortured, or injured, yet the inward man is being renewed by the power of Christ. Paul concludes this impactful section of Scripture with a striking sentiment in 2 Corinthians 12:10, *"For the sake of Christ, then, I am content with weaknesses, insults, hardships, persecutions, and calamities. For when I am weak, then I am strong."*

So how do we find strength when we feel weak? And how do we come to learn the secret of rejoicing in our hardships? We do so by understanding what hardships give us. Too many people have developed the thought that hardships only take from us. But according to the Bible, hardships actually can give something to us as well. It's in this giving to us that we can find the strength to flip the script on adversity and begin to rejoice in our difficulties because our current difficulties can actually propel us closer to Christ. Join me as we take a look at the seven things hardship gives us as found in Paul's letter to the Philippians. We discover these truths within a set of verses found in chapter 1:12-26. The first thing we learn from Paul is that hardship expands the gospel, let's look at verse 12.

Freedom

Hardship Expands the Gospel

"¹²I want you to know, brothers, that what has happened to me has really served to advance the gospel." Philippians 1:12

That's a robust and discerning description from Paul, isn't it? Most people, I would imagine, consider imprisonment, beatings, and such as a negative set of conditions in terms of advancing the gospel. But not Paul, he clearly explains to his readers that the very imprisonment he has endured is cause for a divine expansion of truth. And for that, as we will read later, he counts his entire ordeal as a reason to rejoice. I can almost picture in my mind as some of his very first readers scanned over these lines, they must have thought, "Has Paul gone mad, who in their right mind would welcome persecution and hardships?"

Perhaps it's a good idea to understand a bit more clearly exactly what Paul means when he uses the phrase, *"to advance the gospel."* The word used here for *"advance"* is prokopē (prok-op-ay') which means to have progress or to be advanced by something. This word is used only three times in the New Testament. It's used here in reference to a non-personal thing, meaning the message of the gospel. In the other two places, it's associated on a personal level. It refers to a believer's personal advancement of their faith or spiritual growth. In this setting, however, we understand the phrase to mean something else on a grander and even larger scale.

The core of this Greek word means *"to beat forward"* or *"to lengthen out by hammering"* (as a smith forges metals). Additionally, it carries the idea to cut down that which is in the way. Interestingly, the etymology of the root word is from koptō (kop'-

to), which means "*to cut down.*" This is the exact phrase utilized as a descriptor regarding the triumphal entry of Jesus into Jerusalem. We read of this description in Matthew 21:8, *"Most of the crowd spread their cloaks on the road, and <u>others cut branches from the trees</u> and spread them on the road."*

So, we see these two concepts being explained here by Paul. One, hardships serve to cut down the barriers and provide the very pathway for the message of the Messiah to enter into the hearts of those who are ready to hear. In other words, without an arrest, a shipwreck, and imprisonment, Paul never would have accessed the household of Caesar. His adversity emblematically removed, or cut down, the barriers of the gospel to Rome.

Two, adversity is a methodology in which we are propelled forward as our message of the gospel is lengthened out like a blacksmith who forges his metal. Each blow of the hammer serves the purpose of perpetuating the message stronger and stronger until the whole world knows it. The gospel is driven and advanced forward on the anvil of adversity. That's what Paul is saying here. That's what history has shown. And that's what God wants us to know for our generation as well.

From a personal side, Paul writes, *"I want you to know,"* as he calls out to his brothers. That which has happened to me is of no consequence. What is he saying here? He is saying, "I don't harbor ill-will toward my captures. I don't fault those who may have let me down along the journey. I don't regard my heavenly Father as failing me or forgetting me." He continues, "What *"has happened to me"* hasn't harmed me, it has only aided me, and *"has really served...,"* not me, but *"has really served... to advance the gospel."*

So we now see the first step in understanding how to rejoice in our hardship is to appreciate the clear picture of what Paul is describing here. When you are on the anvil it sure isn't fun, and most times it hurts. It hurts a lot. What God wants you and I to know is that while the adversity you may be experiencing right now is real, even more so is the reality of his message of hope for you and others. It's through our trials and persecutions that many of the obstacles in our way are removed as we are then moved, by the Holy Spirit, into the place of perfection under God's will. As is what transpired in the case of Paul.

Elisabeth Elliot, widow of Jim Elliot, a missionary who lost his life to the very Latin American tribe he was attempting to evangelize, once wrote a summary on this point that I believe to be very beneficial in helping us understand. She wrote,

> "If we do anything to further the kingdom of God, we may expect to find what Christ found on that road - abuse, indifference, injustice, misunderstanding, trouble of some kind. Take it. Why not. To that you were called. In Latin America, someone who feels sorry for himself is said to look like a donkey in a downpour. If we think of the glorious fact that we are on the same path with Jesus, we might see a rainbow."[34]

Shortly after her husband was martyred, Elisabeth practiced what she preached and lived among the very tribe that had killed her husband. Her husband's death became the adversity that cleared the obstacles to the gospel.

Let's take a look at the second truth in helping us to rejoice in our hardship. This principle is much like the first. It's understanding that hardship allows us to evangelize further than before.

T.K. Anderson

Hardship Allows Us to Evangelize Further Than Before

"¹³so that it has become known throughout the whole imperial guard and to all the rest that my imprisonment is for Christ." Philippians 1:13

The greatest Christian evangelist in the 20th Century was, no doubt, Billy Graham. He understood what it took to reach the lost and appreciated the benefit of adversity as it relates to evangelism. Graham once said, "Comfort and prosperity have never enriched the world as much as adversity has."[35] What does he mean by that? I believe he means that there is no greater message to enrich the world than the message of God's love for all humanity. And when we share that message, we are enriching our world, even when, or especially when, adversity is the launching pad through which we share.

Now I want you to think about something for a moment. We know from this story, and from what we read in Acts 28 and Ephesians 6, that Paul was under house arrest in his own rented home. Most likely, it was more like an apartment in a multi-story/multi-family type building. We also know that the Imperial Guard, who was Caesar's personal force, was assigned to guard Paul because he was an important prisoner. He was chained to them, as was the protocol for a prisoner awaiting trial before Caesar. This went on for two years without hindrance.

Yet even in this state, he was able to preach, teach, welcome visitors, and write letters. Including the letter we are looking at today. Most likely, each guard would have been chained to Paul for no more than 8 hours per shift. With three shifts a day to cover his 24-hour-a-day confinement, that would account for over 2,000 opportunities for Paul to present the gospel to these soldiers. I believe this is one of the reasons he would write, *"All the saints greet you, especially those of Caesar's household"* at the end of his correspondence in Philippians 4:22. Paul was a witnessing machine while he was under house arrest. Nothing could stop him. Yet, without the circumstance of his house arrest, these 2,000 opportunities would never have materialized.

Can I share a thought of encouragement with you? If you happen to be going through the middle of a huge battle right now, remember that God uses these very battles to help win the war within the lives of those who are watching you. For example, you may recall a time when you've watched, or heard about, a believer who inspired you. Well, if that's the case, then it may just be your turn to be the inspiration someone else needs at this moment.

When it comes to sharing our faith, Paul is saying that God is more than welcome to use or employ the tough circumstances in his life for those who do not know Christ. Thus, through his hardship, Paul is helping to aid in finding freedom from the heavy burdens, or weight of sin, found in the lives of those God is calling. Which results in a release from the things holding people back.

This, in turn, frees people to become all that God intends them to be. In this case, for Paul, it happened for the Imperial Guards of Rome who received a front row seat to hear the gospel in 8-hour shifts, 24 hours a day, 7 days a week, for 720 days in a row. Here's a good story to illustrate what I'm trying to say.

On October 15, 1997, David Huxley strapped a harness around

his upper torso and attached it to a steel cable some fifteen yards long. The other end of the steel cable was attached to the front-wheel strut of a 747 jetliner that weighed 187 tons. With his tennis shoes firmly planted on the runway, Huxley leaned forward, pulled with all his might, and began moving the jetliner down the runway. He ended up pulling the 747 one hundred yards in one minute and twenty-one seconds.[36]

Wow, what a story! No doubt Mr. Huxley was proud of his "accomplishment." If the goal was to move a machine weighing 187 tons and intended for flying through the air, by foot power alone, then mission accomplished. But 747 jetliners weren't designed to be powered by foot, covering one hundred yards in a little more than a minute. They were designed to soar 30,000 feet in the air at 500 miles per hour. In case you're wondering, that would be 14,000 yards a minute, a far cry from 100 yards a minute! I wonder, how many people are settling for pulling planes instead of flying planes?

As an amazing feat as this seems to be, using brute strength to pull your life along will only get you so far. May I suggest that God designed you to soar with him and to lift your life out of the burdens of this world. It's time to cut the cable and unbuckle the harness that is holding you to the ground. Pulling a plane one hundred yards may sound good, but it's a far cry from its intended design. And so is a life harnessed by sin and tethered to the things of this earth.

With this in mind, picture chain-bound Paul sharing stories and illustrations along with Old Testament prophecies concerning Jesus all entwined with the new teachings of Christ. It's no wonder his impact was so incredible. Guess what? That's what God wants

Freedom

to do in and through your life as well. He wants to take your tragedies, hardships, turmoil, and heartbreaks, and utilize what you're learning and experiencing as a catalyst to propel the gospel message to those who may even be your Imperial Guards.

Are you willing to let God do that? Are you willing to allow your hardships to be utilized to expand the gospel into places and to people who may never have heard it without what you're going through? I hope you are because it will transform your life too. And for that, we can rejoice!

Ok, the third truth in helping us to rejoice in our difficulties is that our hardship is an encouragement to fellow believers. Let's look at verse 14.

Hardship is an Encouragement to Fellow Believers

"14And most of the brothers, having become confident in the Lord by my imprisonment, are much more bold to speak the word without fear." Philippians 1:14

Something happens to a person when you see someone you know, or don't know for that matter, go through something big and yet come out the other side ok. It kind of inspires you a bit, doesn't it? It does for me. When I was a kid, we used to try all sorts of crazy stunts. From dirt bike jumps and snowball fights to cliff jumping and rope swings into a lake, you name we tried it. It's only by God's grace that I came out of those years relatively intact with only two broken bones to show for it. Where did we get the courage to attempt these ill-advised stunts?

Well, in part, if you tuned in to **ABC's Wild World of Sports** from 1971 onward, you're familiar with the opening sequence, in which sportscaster Jim McKay touts "the thrill of victory and the agony of defeat." For nearly three decades, "the agony of defeat" was personified by a ski jumper's spectacular wipeout at Oberstock, Germany. That ski jumper was Vinko Bogataj of Yugoslavia, whose brief presence on the popular show made him the most famous ski jumper in the world, or at least to American sports fans. Over the years, different clips were rotated into the montage to illustrate the "thrill of victory," but Vinko Bogataj's accident remained as the "agony of defeat" through the show's end in 1998.[37]

He would later comment, "Every time I'm on ABC, I crash." But he didn't give up. After the accident, Vinko returned to ski jumping and eventually retired. He did finally achieve success when he coached ski jumper, Franci Petek to become the 1991 Slovenian World Champion.

I share that story with you because there are many times in our life when tragedy, persecution, calamity, or hardship appears to be the very thing that will wipe us out. At the moment it's tempting to give in to the "*agony of defeat*." But what Paul is saying here is my hardship is the very "*thrill of victory*" that is already inspiring others to become more daring for Christ.

Paul uses three words/phrases, to describe for us what his brothers in Christ are experiencing in real-time due to his imprisonment. And these words are not negative, agonizing, defeating or crushing words. These are not *agony of defeat-type* words.

But rather, he uses words that are descriptive of becoming bold,

Freedom

confident and daring for God. These are *thrill of victory-type* words. In fact, these two phrases, *"having become confident in the Lord,"* and, *"are much more bold,"* convey this idea of being *"persuaded to venture out"* into something. It's as if Paul is saying, "Thank God for my imprisonment, because of it my closest friends are convinced to never shy away from anything God is asking them to do. Because we know that no matter what, God is always at our side." We know this last part because Paul ends his little, but powerful, thought with a two-word phrase: *"without fear."*

How do you operate in an environment that is without fear? Simple, you operate without fear if you already know the outcome ahead of time. If you and I are in communion with the Creator of the Universe, who really cares if we're ministering to people from inside or outside a jail cell? If our sharing the very Word of God with people causes us to be locked up, then so be it.

God is in control and I will not be afraid, right? I serve a great King and I'm a citizen of his great Kingdom. That's what Paul is getting across here. When you and I operate in that type of faith, guess what? It inspires other believers as well. It inspires them to get out of their comfort zone and do something daring for God.

Listen, the way we handle adversity and hardship can bring an agony or a thrill to those watching us. So, let me encourage you to stand strong in your hardship, and even though the outside world may view you like the banged-up and broken-down skier, know that God and other believers see the thrill of victory in you as you trust in Jesus to get you through.

For that, we can rejoice!

T.K. Anderson

Ok, we've learned so far that hardship expands the Gospel, allows us to evangelize further than before, and is an encouragement to fellow believers. The fourth truth in helping us to rejoice in our hardship is that it exposes the depth of our friendships. Let's look at verses 15-18.

Hardship Exposes the Depth of Our Friendships

"[15]Some indeed preach Christ from envy and rivalry, but others from goodwill. [16]The latter do it out of love, knowing that I am put here for the defense of the gospel. [17]The former proclaim Christ out of selfish ambition, not sincerely but thinking to afflict me in my imprisonment.[18]What then? Only that in every way, whether in pretense or in truth, Christ is proclaimed, and in that I rejoice."
Philippians 1:15-18

It would be very difficult to go through life without friends. Some would say it would be practically impossible and not near half the fun. Friends are what make life bearable in many cases and as we go through life it's the friendships with the greatest depth where we find the greatest richness and reward.

"There is nothing better than a friend, children's author, Linda Grayson, writes, …unless it is a friend with chocolate."

I don't know Linda Grayson, but maybe she's on to something. Truth be told, however, when we find a friend, preferably with chocolate, that has stood the test of time, we understand the depth of our connection is far stronger than the hardships attempting to pull our life apart. Life teaches us these deep, rich, and mature friendships don't happen overnight.

Aristotle had this in mind when he wrote, "Wishing to be friends is quick work, but friendship is a slow ripening fruit."

And it was C.S. Lewis who wrote in his book, The Four Loves, that "Friendship ... is born at the moment when one man says to another, 'What! You too? I thought that no one but myself...'"

God designed us to connect with each other. Connection is good. It's healthy. It's part of the plan of God for our lives. But how do we know just who to connect with? How do we jettison those who may not be a true benefit to us in the long term? Can God actually help us in this process? Well according to Paul's story, the answer is yes. Not only can he, but he does.

As Paul was sitting under house arrest, he mentions two sets of friends. Those who continue to minister on his behalf *"out of love"* for Paul and his condition, and those who continue to preach the gospel *"out of selfish ambition."* And what caused this revelation of differing friendship? Right, the very hardship Paul was enduring. One group was trying to afflict him while the other group was trying to assist him.

Paul was happy either way because this separation of true friendship from selfish friendship aided him in vetting out those who he could really count on. That's what hardship and adversity do for us. It's a way for God to help us in revealing those who have *"goodwill"* toward us and are *"sincerely"* concerned about our suffering. And for that, we can rejoice!

The flip side to this point is for us to consider our motives. How are we treating those we know who are going through hardship? It's a sobering question, isn't it? Are we ministering out of love and goodwill or are we ministering out of ambition and pretense? Only the Holy Spirit knows the true motives of our heart, but this point is very piercing as we evaluate our internal motives for ministry.

To sum up this point, Paul rejoices either way. It doesn't bother him if people are ministering the gospel with great motives or not-so-great motives. For Paul, the hardship reveals the motives so he can then focus on those who are true friends. And the others? He just leaves it in God's hands and trusts that God will sort that out in the end. But if ministry is taking place, Paul is for that!

Continuing in our message, the fifth lesson for us to learn in how to rejoice through adversity is to remember that hardship brings explosive growth to our personal walk.

Hardship Brings Explosive Growth to Our Personal Walk

"Yes, and I will rejoice, [19]for I know that through your prayers and the help of the Spirit of Jesus Christ this will turn out for my deliverance [20]as it is my eager expectation and hope that I will not be at all ashamed, but that with full courage now as always Christ will be honored in my body, whether by life or by death." Phil 1:18-20

Some of the most explosive growth on our planet happens in the world of trees. Arborists tell us two types of tree growth are very impressive. Some species of Bamboo are actually capable of sprouting up to 4 inches per day. The fastest-growing Bamboo, and world record holder, sprouted 35 inches in a single day.[38] Although tall, the roots go about 10 inches deep. However, the giant sequoia given good conditions and gardening skills will grow

Freedom

2 feet a year and increase its trunk diameter by 4 inches. Reaching a trunk diameter of 34 feet by its 100th year.[39] The average sequoia is over 200 feet tall, and its root system can occupy over 1 acre of earth containing 90,000 cubic feet of soil. That's called explosive growth with strong and stable roots. This illustration brings us to a question. How can we repeat that type of result in our personal walk with Christ?

I don't know if you caught it or not, but if you look closely, Paul uses the expression, *"I will rejoice,"* two times in a row in verse 18. In a back-to-back format, Paul is shouting from the pages of his letter that no matter the circumstances, he is going to rejoice. The reason for this confidence is rooted in his knowing that through the prayers of those in Philippi and through *"the help of the Spirit of Jesus Christ this will turn out for his deliverance."* His confidence is strong, and his expectation is off the charts.

He is a wonderful example for us. It's like he has acquired some type of super spiritual strength not common to normal everyday Christians. When I see this type of courage in the Bible, I naturally ask myself where did this come from and how can I get it? Are you like me as well? Do you ask that too? Do you crave for a stronger personal walk with Christ?

It's fair to say Paul experienced explosive growth in his walk with Christ over the years. It wasn't bamboo-type growth it was more like sequoia-type growth. If we take just this one story, we see a man who is a far cry from the man 25 to 30 years early who rejected Christ and was instead the very one causing the persecution he is now experiencing. In Acts chapters 8 and 9 we gain an understanding of how far away Paul was from the gospel.

He is described as the one who *"approved of [Stephen's] execution"* and ravaged the church in Jerusalem. Acts 8:3 continues to say he, *"enter[ed] house after house, he dragged off men and women and committed them to prison."* In chapter 9 we see Paul *"breathing threats and murder against the disciples of the Lord."* This is a man who is lost, angry, deceived, blinded, and causing great harm to the Body of Christ. How could there be any hope for him?

Yet, we see the grace of God enter the scene and everything changes as Paul encounters Christ in chapter 9 of the book of Acts. From that moment on, until this moment captured for us in a Roman jail cell, Paul had endured tremendous hardship. It was through these two decade-long continuations of adversity, hardship, testing, and persecution that his walk with Christ continued to grow. His spiritual roots went deep and wide as the trunk of his influence expanded year after year after year. Until finally, what once was a seedling of faith back in Acts chapter nine, is now similar to a 200-foot giant sequoia of a man sold out for Christ in every imaginable way possible.

Know this; the hardship, adversity, persecution, trial, or difficulty you may be facing today is there, in part, to cause explosive growth in your personal walk with Christ. You may not see it today, but as you learn to lean into more of God and as you learn to trust his plan deeper, your roots are growing stronger, and your influence is expanding. God is using hardships to build up your courage and expectation so that you can say as Paul said in this verse, *"I will not be at all ashamed, but that with full courage now as always Christ will be honored."* And for that, I think we can all agree to rejoice!

We have learned that hardship expands the Gospel, allows us to evangelize further than before, is an encouragement to fellow believers, exposes the depth of our friendships, and brings explosive growth to our walk with Christ. The sixth truth for us to learn is that hardship exhibits true motives.

Hardship Exhibits True Motives

"*[21]For to me to live is Christ, and to die is gain.*" Philippians 1:21

When researching this book, I discovered there are many differing opinions about life and its meaning. A quick Google search for the phrase "quotes about life" yielded over 13 billion results in half a second. Clearly, there is no shortage of commentary regarding the purpose of life and our motives attached to it. What does it mean to live? I mean really live? Many people claim to know the answer.

"Go confidently in the direction of your dreams! Live the life you've imagined," Henry David Thoreau famously wrote. "*The purpose of our lives is to be happy,*" says the Dalai Lama. Aristotle weighed in by writing: *"It is during our darkest moments that we must focus to see the light."* And pop culture artist Bob Marley said: *"Love the life you live. Live the life you love."* So, which is it? Can we really find long-lasting fulfillment and purpose by focusing on something as fleeting as personal happiness or as nebulous as Aristotle's "*see the light?*"

The purpose of this chapter isn't to examine the greatest philosophies of life, but to notice that it's through the experience of hardship, at least for Paul, that his true motive for life was brought to the forefront. He couldn't be clearer in his assessment of life by writing, *"to live is Christ, and to die is gain."* That's the interesting thing about trials and struggles, they seem to function as an automatic filter that strips away the irrelevant things in our life.

In fact, if you are going through a rough time as you read this, you're feeling the truth of this filter in real-time. The same was true for Paul. But this wasn't a new truth for Paul. As divine providence would have it, five years earlier, Paul wrote a similar thought: *"For if we live, we live to the Lord, and if we die, we die to the Lord. So then, whether we live or whether we die, we are the Lord's"* Romans 14:8. Did you catch who he wrote this to? You guessed it, to the believers in Rome! That's an interesting twist to say the least.

History tells us Paul wrote his letter to the Romans in 56-57 A.D. while in Corinth. Could it be God was already preparing the ground for his eventual arrival in the Imperial City? God only knows the answer to that question, but one thing is for certain, hard times prioritize our focus and prepare us for our eternal destiny.

As a follower of Christ, it's a focus not looking for personal happiness, individual achievements, or hoping to grasp the cosmic meaning of reality one day as we stare into the depths of space. But rather, it's a laser focus on living each day for Christ and allowing our hardships to tear away the facades of this temporal life. And for that, we can rejoice.

It's no wonder Paul could write a postscript to the believers in Ephesus, just before the letter we're focusing on in this chapter, that focused solely on proclaiming the most important message the world has ever heard, *"[pray that] words may be given to me in opening my mouth boldly to proclaim the mystery of the gospel,* [20] *for which I am an ambassador in chains, that I may declare it boldly, as I ought to speak."* (Ephesians 6:19-20)

We've covered that hardship expands the Gospel, allows us to evangelize further than before, is an encouragement to fellow believers, exposes the depth of our friendships, brings explosive growth to our walk with Christ, and exhibits true motives. The seventh and final truth for us to learn is hardship equips us for the future. Let's look at verses 22 through 26 in Philippians chapter one.

Hardship Equips Us for the Future

"22If I am to live in the flesh, that means fruitful labor for me. Yet which I shall choose I cannot tell. 23I am hard-pressed between the two. My desire is to depart and be with Christ, for that is far better. 24But to remain in the flesh is more necessary on your account. 25Convinced of this, I know that I will remain and continue with you all, for your progress and joy in the faith, 26so that in me you may have ample cause to glory in Christ Jesus, because of my coming to you again." Philippians 1:22-26

The phrase 'win-win' was created in the 1960s within the communal society of northern California and popularized by Stephen Covey's 1989 best-seller, *The 7 Habits of Highly Effective People*. To date, Covey's book has sold more than 30 million copies worldwide. There's a good chance you're familiar with this term. It's a phrase synonymous with winning with either choice a person has to make in a two-sided decision-making process. For example: Should I go to In and Out or should I go to McDonald's for lunch? Either way, I win, right? That's the underlying idea here.

If Paul stays alive and continues his ministry, he wins. If Paul is executed by Nero and is transported to Heaven, he also wins. It's the ultimate 'win-win' situation unique to those who are followers of Jesus Christ.

You can sense a pull in Paul's voice between his leadership and his longing. He has a deep pull in his heart for the people of God and his responsibility as their spiritual leader. Yet, he has deep desire to finally be with the Lord. After we've been through the filtering process of hardship, we are prepared for the future in either direction. Once the façade of this world is stripped away and our true motives are revealed, we can see clearly the two choices available to the child of God. Stay and continue the ministry God has for us or, in His divine plan, meet the Lord face to face for all eternity. What a wonderful and glorious future, either way! It's truly a 'win-win' for each of us.

But how do we get to this place of 'win-win' when everything and everyone around us seems to be pulling us to look after our own affairs? Look after number one, the world tells us. Your future is what you make it. It can be so confusing. Paul understood with absolute clarity that the presence of God is all in all. Perhaps what that Psalmist wrote, *"You, (Lord), make known to me the path of life; in your presence there is fullness of joy; at your right hand are pleasures forevermore"*[40] was on the wall of Paul's jail cell. I have no idea if that's true or not. But most likely, it was written on the wall of his heart!

Look, I'm not an unbelieving science fiction writer but if I was, I would write a title for this set of verses in Philippians one that says, The Future of My Future. Because if I wasn't a believer, that's what this sounds like. But, as followers of Jesus, we don't have to look at this from some type of magical or mystical point of view. We know that our current hardships are only preparing us for our eventual time with Christ.

In fact, we catch a glimpse of this transforming thought in Paul's letter to the Corinthians, *"²For in this tent we groan, longing to put on our heavenly dwelling… ⁸Yes, we are of good courage, and we would rather be away from the body and at home with the Lord."* (2 Corinthians 5:2, 5:8)

Theologian N.T. Wright explains this as our "life after life after death" in his explanation of what happens to believers in glorified bodies during and after our Millennial reign with Christ. He writes: "Heaven is the place where God's purposes for the future are stored up. It isn't where they are meant to stay so that one would need to go to heaven to enjoy them; it is where they are kept safe against the day when they will become a reality on earth."[41] This, of course, is in reference to Peter's words in his letter referring, *"to an inheritance that is imperishable, undefiled, and unfading, kept in heaven for you."* (1 Peter 1:4)

I know this last point feels like drinking from a theological fire hose and I don't have the necessary time to explain the totality of the point here, but suffice it to say, the big lesson for us in Paul's letter regarding hardships is that we have a future glory awaiting us. And as we wait for that ultimate future with Christ, for as long as He wants us here, we will continue to live out the future He has in store for us here…in humble obedience. When we arrive to the moment of our leaving, may we have the same confidence as Paul when he wrote: *"For I am already being poured out as a drink offering, and the time of my departure has come."* (2 Timothy 4:6)

Conclusion

We started this chapter by looking at an obscure verse tucked away in the Old Testament book of Job, *"Hard times and trouble are God's way of getting our attention!"* (Job 36:15) We learned from this that the very difficulties we try to avoid can work to our advantage in a way that only God can design. From Paul's letter we discovered there are seven reasons to rejoice in our hardships, and with this new-found action plan, we are better prepared to face the future difficulties that come our way.

Yet, even with this knowledge, handling difficulties can be challenging and unrelenting unless we train our focus on the greater context that is occurring through our adversities. I'll leave this chapter with a closing story that has helped me understand this entire discussion with greater clarity.

In the 1800s, a group of women met to study the Bible in Dublin. They were puzzled by the words of Malachi 3:3, "And he shall sit as a refiner and purifier of silver." One of the ladies promised to call on a silversmith and report to them what he said on the subject. She went accordingly, and without telling the object of her errand, begged to know the process of refining silver which he fully described to her. "But sir," said she, "Do you sit while the work of refining is going on?"

"Oh yes, Madam," replied the silversmith, "I must sit with my eye steadily fixed on the furnace. For if the time necessary for refining be exceeded in the slightest degree, the silver is sure to be injured."

At once she saw the beauty and comfort of the expression, "He shall sit as a refiner and purifier of silver." Christ sees it needful to put His children into the furnace, but He is seated by the side of it. His eye is steadily intent on the work of purifying, and His wisdom and love are both engaged in the best manner for His children. Their trials do not come at random.

As the lady was leaving the shop the silversmith called her back and said he had still further to mention that he only knew when the process of purifying was complete by seeing his own image reflected in the silver. When Christ's image is reflected in us his work of purifying is accomplished.[42]

T.K. Anderson

Chapter Five

Rejoice in Humility

Philippians 2:1-11

One of Aesop's well-known fables concerned a turtle who envied the ducks who swam in the pond where he lived. As he listened to them describe the wonders of the world they had seen, he was filled with a great desire to travel. But being a turtle, he was unable to travel far. Finally, two ducks offered to help him. One of the ducks said, "We will each hold an end of a stick in our mouths. You hold the stick in the middle in your mouth, and we will carry you through the air so that you can see what we see when we fly. But be quiet or you will be sorry." The turtle loved the idea. He took hold of the stick and away into the sky they went.

The ducks flew up above the trees and circled around the meadow. The turtle was amazed and overjoyed at his new perspective on the world. He marveled at the flowers on the hillside. Just then a cagey old crow flew past. Astonished at the sight of a turtle flying through the air carried by two ducks he said, "Surely this must be the king of all turtles!" "Why certainly…" the turtle began—but as he opened his mouth to speak, he lost his grip on the stick and fell fast to the ground below.[43]

"Pride goes before destruction and a haughty spirit before a fall," the Bible says. While there are times to enjoy the heights of

our success, more frequently than not, we find ourselves in trouble because we focus entirely too much on our activities, accomplishments, and achievements instead of maintaining a quiet sense of humility. The Bible explains it this way: *"Even a fool, when he holds his peace, is counted wise; and he who shuts his lips is esteemed a man of understanding." (*Proverbs 17:28)

Yet, some may ask aren't there times when having self-confidence in our achievements can be good? Or isn't it good to hold on to a sense of importance in our world, especially in the plan God has for my life? Wouldn't that be a good case where pride, or self-confidence, can be deemed virtuous?

Author Leon Seltzer tackles this delicate dichotomy by writing, "Ironically, pride might be likened to a fantastical double-edged sword, with a harmless rubber tip on one end and a destructive, razor-sharp blade on the other. Staying with this metaphor, the stinging, pointed-edge side can easily 'cut' others—and therefore injure relationships to the point they're irreparable."[44]

That's the side of the sword we're talking about here in Philippians chapter two of our study. In the first eleven verses of this famous passage of Scripture, we find three incredible truths regarding humility and how we can best access a specially designed gift of God in our personal relationships, business dealings, and daily interactions with those around us.

As Paul finds himself in a very humble location, *a Roman jail cell*, he knows his apostolic letter to fellow believers will be very impactful when finally read. Yet, he knows these words will fly in complete opposition to his world, as they still do today. Paul knows it will be a hard-hitting read.

Freedom

He begins chapter two of his letter by calling his readers to a great quest. It's a quest for humility. Then he provides a key to unlock our greatest potential while putting away one of our fiercest enemies. Finally, Paul embarks on one of the most beautiful passages in all of Scripture that provides the ultimate example of how we can, and should, delight in humility. And for that, Paul concludes, we can rejoice.

The first truth that causes us to rejoice in the quest for humility is that it results in unity. Let's look at verses one and two in Philippians chapter two.

The Quest for Humility Results in Unity

"¹So if there is any encouragement in Christ, any comfort from love, any participation in the Spirit, any affection and sympathy, ²complete my joy by being of the same mind, having the same love, being in full accord and of one mind." Philippians 2:1-2

Generally, the purpose of a great quest is to find something special at the end of the line. Or perhaps to achieve some type of liberating goal or beneficial objective. Famous quests in literature would be J.R.R. Tolkien's, **Lord of the Rings**, C.S. Lewis', **Chronicles of Narnia**, or George Lucas', **Star Wars**. In each of these creative stories the forces of good eventually win the day as characters battle the forces of evil in a quest to overcome their adversaries.

Similarly, that's what Paul is laying out for his readers in the opening sentence of chapter two. He begins with this small phrase, *"So if there is any..."* and then continues to lay out five resources available to us as followers of Christ as we embark on the journey of shadowing our Savior.

This phrase, *so if there is any,"* is an expression that might as well say, *"because there is."* It's not like Paul is wondering if there is any encouragement and comfort, or the rest of the items on his list. It's the exact opposite. It's precisely because there are five resources available to us that we can achieve the unity desired by God for His children. We can and should complete this quest.

For example, looking back to our literary illustrations of great quests, there's always some type of resource or special means by which the forces of good can achieve their mission. For Tolkien, it was the **One Ring**. For Lewis, it was the **Rhindon Sword**. For Lucas, it was the Jedi's **Light Saber**. As impressive as these resources appear on the big screen, they serve as an insignificant token in comparison to the special means we have available to us.

It seems to me that our problem with discovering how to live a life rooted in humility is not due to a lack of resources, or divine power, but rather due to a limitation in our biblical data and anticipation of what God can do through us.

A. B. Simpson, who was a well-known late 19th / early 20th Century Canadian preacher, theologian, and founder of the Christian and Missionary Alliance presented it this way, *"Our God has boundless resources. The only limit is in us. Our asking, our thinking, and our praying are too small. Our expectations are too limited."*[45] Another way to put it is, if your quest is too big, if your resources are too limited, if your strategy is too narrow, then perhaps your God is too small!

Freedom

In one of his Old Testament commentaries, the famed Christian communicator, J. Vernon McGee, shared the following first-hand experience: "Right before World War II, the city of Pasadena was having its annual Rose Parade. The float that was entered by the Standard Oil Company was covered with American Beauty roses. It was a sight to behold. The theme of the parade was, "Be prepared." Right in the middle of the parade, the Standard Oil Company's float ran out of gas. It stopped right where I was viewing the parade.

I couldn't help but laugh. If there was one float that should not have run out of gas, it was that one. Standard Oil Company should have had plenty of gas! As I looked at the float, I saw a picture of many Christians today. They are beautiful, but they have no power in their lives. They have beauty and prestige, but no power."[46]

What Paul is saying here in his opening section is that we are not alone on our quest to live in humility. A quest that leads us to unity. But rather, we have actual power, authentic resources, and real, tangible fuel to power our spiritual and relational engines. So, what are these amazing resources available to us?

Looking back to the text we see five specific resources listed, as we journey out into this new quest. These five resources will help us be successful on our hero's journey. It's a journey of biblical faith.

It starts with an understanding that we acquire an *"Encouragement in Christ"* when we become a Christian. The word used for encouragement is linked to the same word Jesus used in John 14:16 when he explained that we have a Helper (Comforter, Advocate, Intercessor, or Counselor) in the person of the Holy

Spirit. This *"encouragement"* isn't a reference to having Jesus as a personal cheerleader or divine life coach. It's not a reference to having someone who stands on the sidelines of our experiences, shouting words of affirmation and support to us. It's way more forceful than that.

This is a very robust and deep concept rooted in the idea of individual and corporate connection to God himself through the very presence of God in our lives. We have a Comforter that now dwells within us. *"And I will ask the Father and he will give you another Helper, to be with you forever."* (John 14:16) That my friend, is a very powerful resource.

Next, we come to realize that we have available a *"comfort from love."* At first glance, this seems to be some type of mushy statement or lighthearted quality. But nothing could be further from the truth. In the original language, this actual statement is more akin to holding a logical fortitude, resonating deep with our soul, that all is well between our life and God.

We catch a piece of this type of thought in some of the old hymns. For example, A famous hymn written in 1876 by Horatio Spafford captures this brilliantly. He wrote this famous song during a time of great pain in his life. The Great Chicago Fire in 1871 destroyed much of his property investments and left him broke. He was hit even harder by the economic downturn of 1873.

Ahead of a planned family trip to Europe in 1873, Spafford had to stay behind to attend to some business. He sent his four daughters and his wife ahead. Their ship collided with another vessel and sank. He received word from his wife via this short telegram: I was "saved alone…"

Freedom

As he later traveled to meet his wife, he was inspired to write this legendary hymn as a painful meditation as his ship passed over the location where his daughters lost their lives.[47] This is how Horatio Spafford described what it meant to have a *"comfort from love."*

> *When peace, like a river, attendeth my way,*
> *When sorrows like sea billows roll;*
> *Whatever my lot, thou has taught me to say,*
> *It is well, it is well, with my soul.*

According to the Bible, this is a resource that we have available to us as members of God's family. And when we get ahold of this and allow it to penetrate our hearts, it won't matter what comes our way because we will be sheltered in Christ alongside the temporal pains of this life. When we get God's love. I mean really get it. It revolutionizes our perspective. A deep resolve overtakes us, and we have comfort, consolation, support, or dare I say foundation on account of his love for us.

Continuing to follow the text, Paul says next we enjoy a *"participation in the Spirit."* Have you ever visited a friend's house and needed to tap into their Wi-Fi network? Once they share their passcode with you, boom, you're in and you're logged into the same network. That's a parallel idea here Paul is communicating. When we get saved and sealed by the Holy Spirit, we become a part of the Body of Christ. Through this connectivity, we have a grand participation with fellow believers across the globe. It's like having a spiritual network we can log into any time we want.

Finally, the last two resources for us are listed as a type of twin benefits. According to the text, we hold both *"affection and sympathy"* from God, and toward others.

Mother Teresa summed up our relationship with others this way, *"If you judge people, you have no time to love them."* However, comedian Steve Martin held a different take on the topic, *"Before you criticize a man, walk a mile in his shoes. That way, when you do criticize him, you'll be a mile away and have his shoes."* I think there's a bit of wisdom in both approaches. But it appears Dietrich Bonhoeffer hit the nail on the head when he wrote, *"We must learn to regard people less in the light of what they do or omit to do, and more in the light of what they suffer."*[48]

Your ability to empathize with the suffering of another one of God's children is actually a resource for you on the road to unity through humility. Connecting through pain lets the other person know they are not alone. Many times, that's the only thing holding us together. At that moment, we become the tangible hands and feet of Jesus to our brothers and sisters in the most desperate of times. This type of understanding builds unity while simultaneously illustrating for us the very hand of God toward us as indicated in a very famous song.

"He's Got the Whole World in His Hands" is a traditional African American spiritual, first published in 1927. In 1953, Marian Anderson sang the song before a live television audience of 60 million people on NBC and CBS, as part of Ford's 50th Anniversary Show. It became an international hit in 1957 by English singer Laurie London and the first and only gospel song to hit #1 on a U.S. pop singles chart.[49]

If you're like me, you remember singing this song in Sunday School, Vacation Bible School, or at night with your parents or grandparents. It's a simple song, with simple lyrics, but it carries a wonderfully powerful spiritual punch. It's a song that reminds us God's smiling down on us and no matter our trouble, or no matter our turmoil, He's got the whole world in His hands. It's a humble reminder that the deepest of truths can be best explained in the simplest of words. It prompts me to recall the story of a little boy who once asked his mom about God's chin.

One day a young boy said to mother, "Mommy, the whole world is God's chin, isn't it?" When his mother asked him, "Why are you asking?" He responded, "The whole world is under His smile, so it must be God's chin, right?"

This metaphor of being *"under God's smile"* is an amazingly simple way for us sophisticated *'adults'* to understand. When we take time to slow down and think it through, it leads us to catch the revelation of the Father's personal affection toward each of us.

These five resources of encouragement, comfort, participation, affection, and sympathy give us the tools necessary to complete the journey set out before us. Skillfully pivoting from verse one to verse two in the text, Paul lists four results as we utilize these five resources set aside for us. He continues by writing, *"complete my joy by being of the same mind, having the same love, being in full accord and of one mind."* (Philippians 2:2)

It's clear to see, the result of utilizing our resources guides us down the path toward unity. So, we can see, according to the opening verses of this beautiful passage, the quest for humility results in unity, and for that, according to Paul, we can rejoice!

Paul doesn't stop here however; he continues in this expedition toward rejoicing through humility by showing us the key of humility removes our vanity. Let's take a look at verses three and four.

The Key of Humility Removes our Vanity

"³Do nothing from selfish ambition or conceit, but in humility count others more significant than yourselves. ⁴Let each of you look not only to his own interest but also to the interests of others." Phil 2:3-4

In Muhammad Ali's heyday, as the heavyweight champion in boxing, he had taken his seat on a 747 which was starting to taxi down the runway for takeoff. The flight attendant walked by and noticed the Champ didn't have his seatbelt on, and said, "Please fasten your seatbelt, sir." Ali looked up proudly and snapped, "Superman don't need no seatbelt." Without hesitation, the flight attendant stared at him and said, "Superman don't need no plane."[50]

It's easy to get caught up in our own image, isn't it? We have a propensity to think pretty highly of ourselves at times, don't we? We live in a day and age where we are encouraged to look after ourselves, at the expense of others. "Put your own needs first," "Do what's right for me," and "Fake it till you make it" are common mantras in our generation. We've mastered all of this on social media.

Why do you think social media has such a draw? We can create a life that is completely implausible. We manufacture a narrative for the world and then log in daily to see all the good things people are saying about us. Or if we're a bit less narcissistic, we live

Freedom

vicariously through the lives of others. And if we lose our shyness just a bit, we don't bother worrying about leaving behind our personal commentary regarding someone else's life. Most of which is not complimentary, of course. Strange how we find glee in sharing our opinion on the profile of a complete stranger, isn't it?

So, exactly how many people have descended into the daily trap of social media? According to the data, compiled by pewresearch.org, close to 80% of American's use social media frequently. Of that group, some 60% to 70% of them use it daily, with sites like Facebook, YouTube, Snapchat, and Instagram leading the pack.[51]

However, according to the Bible, when we are humble, we tend to not think about ourselves too much. I for one think that's probably a good thing. Let me put it this way, if vanity is a joy killer, then humility is a vanity destroyer. Another way to look at humility is the vaccine against the virus of selfishness. But here's the kicker, if we start looking out for the interests of others, the Bible says we'll experience true joy. Remember Paul's words in verse two? He wrote, *"Complete my joy."* This portion of scripture, in verses three and four, is simply a continuation of the original thought he began just eighteen words ago. And it brings up a good question, how do we live a joyful life?

Tom Brady, a seven-time Super Bowl-winning quarterback, sat down and spoke with NFL writer, Peter King, in August of 2021 for the edition of Football Morning in America. During the 20-minute discussion, Brady took issue with athletes blaming others when things don't go their way. "Today, the world wants to blame, and shame, and guilt, and fear everything all the time," Brady told King.

"We would never teach our kids that, we would never say, 'This is how you're gonna get through life the best — you're gonna blame everyone when things don't go right.' Or 'I always get it my way but you should never get it your way.' It's not how to live a joyful life."[52]

According to Tom Brady, one of the ways to live a joyful life is, don't blame others for your problems. I think I'd agree with him on that. And why not? We sure could use more joyful people in our culture, but what does the Bible say about how to live a joyful life?

Should Christians even focus on it? We've all heard stories about cranky Christians. Grumpy Gus, sad Suzi, and irritable Irene can clear out a church lobby in a flash, no doubt about it. I wish they weren't so unlikable because that's not the way Christians should be. Did you know words like "rejoice," "be glad," "joy," and "joyful" occur hundreds of times in the Bible, and a grumpy Christian is actually a contradiction in terms. The Bible says we should, *"Rejoice always,"* in 1 Thessalonians 5:16.

"Oh, but the world I live in is a mess," the cranky person might say. Well, guess what? We aren't called to complain about what's happening in the world. Last time I checked, there are zero rewards in heaven for complaining. There's no such thing as a Complainer's Crown in the Bible, believe me I've looked.

Billy Graham said, "We're to do all we can to make the world a better place—and over the centuries Christians have done exactly that. God calls us to love others for the sake of Christ—and then to put our love into action."[53]

God told the Israelites, who were prisoners in a foreign land, to

Freedom

"seek the peace and prosperity of the city to which I have carried you into exile. Pray to the Lord for it." (Jeremiah 29:7) So that's our job, to be salt and light in the world.

Why is it then that Christians have a hard time being joyful? Consider this, florists create packages of seeds labeled "gorgeous purple," "exceedingly beautiful," "remarkably fine," and so on, referring to the flowers. But if these seeds get into the hands of an untrained person who has never nurtured flowers or if they are planted in cold, wet, desolate soil, and at an untimely season, then only a few of them will sprout, coming up slowly, colorless, and uninspiring. They will be neglected, and the weeds will choke them. And when the time for blooming comes, there will be one or two miserable flowers, and people will say. "I knew this florist was a hypocrite. Ha, look at the result. Look at the descriptions. It's all a big hoax."

Yet we all know it's how a seed is planted, the preparation of the soil, and the season that matters. Similarly, because people know Christianity is "joy producing," they conclude when they become Christians they'll automatically be transported into a mystical joyful experience. They suppose they just "breathe it in" as they would oxygen and some type of magnificent "Divine Fragrance of Joy" will overtake them constantly this side of heaven. While it may be true in our conversion experience, the truth is, it doesn't work like that in our everyday life. The reason there is not more joy in the Church is because we don't know how to plant the seeds and develop the flowers.

Paul is encouraging us in this pair of verses to plant deeply into the soil of humility and when we do, we will harvest joy as promised us by the Lord. We plant into this soil by carrying out two positive actions and two curative actions as described in the text.

What are the positive actions?
- *Count others more significant than yourselves*
- *Look...to the interests of others*

What are the curative actions?
- *Do nothing from selfish ambition*
- *Do nothing from conceit*

We can view the two positive actions as seeds being placed into the soil of humility. We can view the two curative actions as the nurturing of those seeds as our spiritual life begins to grow. The promise to us is simple. As we follow this spiritual gardening strategy, we will unlock the key to humility while we experience true unity. And for that, according to Paul, we can rejoice!

Ok, so we've looked at how the quest for humility results in unity and how the key of humility removes our vanity. Next, Paul shows us how the Christ of humility retains all authority. This, by far, will be the greatest lesson of all. Let's read through all of the verses, five through eleven.

The Christ of Humility Retains All Authority

"⁵Have this mind among yourselves, which is yours in Christ Jesus, ⁶ who, though he was in the form of God, did not count equality with God a thing to be grasped, but emptied himself, by taking the form of a servant, being born in the likeness of men. ⁸And being found in human form, he humbled himself by becoming obedient to the point of death, even death on a cross.

⁹Therefore God has highly exalted him and bestowed on him the name that is above every name, ¹⁰so that at the name of Jesus every knee should bow, in heaven and on earth and under the earth, ¹¹and every tongue confess that Jesus Christ is Lord, to the glory of God the Father." Philippians 2:5-11

There's a wonderful narrative regarding this passage I recently found, "These verses are very likely a hymn or poem that Paul wrote or borrowed as an illustration. They offer Jesus as the perfect role model for Christian unity. While the story of the cross is recorded in the Gospels and explained in the New Testament letters, only this passage views the crucifixion through the eyes of the Lord Himself. It presents a glimpse of His perspective so that His followers might see the price of unity: His death."[54]

Yet it was through His death that He has now been highly exalted. I don't have enough room in this chapter to develop a full explanation of the beautiful description of Christ found within this passage. But I can say in summary, verses five through eight describe for us the pattern of servanthood found within the humanity of Christ that we can achieve as His followers. Meaning, within His humanity the servanthood of Christ was a real thing He managed.

It's important to remember, Jesus didn't have some type of superhero waiver of what it means to put away human ambition, passion, or desire. But He did, and He did so willingly, knowingly, and effectively. Instead of a waiver, He showed us what it means to waive our rights, rights that we so proudly like to express. This entire point is perfectly laid out for us at the start of verse five, *"Have this mind among yourselves, which is yours in Christ Jesus."*

What Paul means by this, is that obtaining unity, through servanthood, is entirely up to us.

It becomes a part of our actions toward each other. It's entirely attainable. This phrase is given to us as an imperative in the original language. Meaning it's something that should be viewed as a directive. Something that can be done by the reader. Like when your doctor tells you, "It's imperative for you to take this medicine every day." It's something you can do and it's something you should do.

Now, moving through the text, verses nine through eleven explain the post- resurrection reality after Christ's ascension. Paul explains a coming exaltation of Jesus both in heaven and upon the earth. You see when Christ came to earth the first time, He willingly exchanged His robes of royalty for our cloak of sin.

In doing so, He created a way for us to exchange our filthy rags for a garment of praise. Isaiah 64:6 puts it this way, *"We have all become like one who is unclean, and all our righteous deeds are like a polluted garment."* Yet, a few chapters earlier, in 61:3, the prophet Isaiah wrote we will be given, *"a garment of praise instead of a spirit of despair."* He goes on to say that we, *"will be called oaks of righteousness, a planting of the LORD for the display of his splendor."* What a wonderful reminder and beautiful promise for those who follow Christ.

The phrase *garment of praise* is a metaphor for the gladness and thanksgiving God's people feel when they are filled with the joy of the Lord. In ancient times, it was customary for a grieving person to wear a sackcloth Esther 4:1. The garment of praise is the opposite of sackcloth; it is brightly colored attire, symbolic of celebration. The Christian Standard Bible translates it as "splendid clothes."

Isaiah 61:3 speaks of a garment of praise in a prophecy that the coming Messiah would, *"provide for those who grieve in Zion."* The Lord promises that He would *"bestow on them a crown of beauty instead of ashes, the oil of joy instead of mourning, and a garment of praise instead of a spirit of despair."*[55]

So how do we pull all this together? How about like this, if we want true joy in our life, we should walk every day in the awareness of the majesty of our Savior. Simply put, this is His world. This is His universe. My life is His life to direct. This is His Kingdom to rule. I'm just a servant and He is my King.

Jesus came to earth the first time as the suffering servant, but when He returns the second time, He will come as the righteous King to establish His Kingdom.

When you and I get our lives in alignment with the King of Kings and the Lord of Lords, and we recognize who's the only One truly in charge of it all, it brings us joy. Why? Because we know that He knows how it all plays out in the end. How does it all play out? He wins! And if He wins, then we win!

Imagine for a moment, right now you received a text message from your bank saying, "You won $100 million." At first, you wouldn't believe it, but then if you called your bank, verified it, double-checked it and all that, if you truly found out that you had just won $100 million, and the money had been transferred into your account, how do you think you'd feel right now? Seriously, how do you think you'd feel? Pretty happy, right? Rejoicing a little bit? Maybe joyful? Maybe even full of joy? You'd stop working, wouldn't you?

And why? Because you'd have a bit of control over your finances, right? You'd be confident in your future; you'd be less worried about the unexpected. You might even want to share that confidence with those around you and spread the joy to others, right? Of course, you would. It would be natural.

Now, if you think about it, if you've been saved, you've won something way more valuable than $100 million. You've been given eternal life. You've been given true purpose, peace, and prosperity. When you know who Christ is and how far His authority reaches, then you know $100 million pales in comparison to the control our King has over our life and this world, both now and forevermore.

When we comprehend this, walk in this, meditate on this, contemplate this, share this, discuss this, and repeat it over and over again. This is the source of our joy because we know, beyond a shadow of a doubt that our future is secure, our present is manageable, and our past is forgiven. We don't have to fret about the temporary things of this world, because our King is coming again to take us home to be with Him forever. And that is a good thing, and that gives us great cause to rejoice!

So, seek humility and be full of joy because He is in control. And for that, according to Paul, we can rejoice!

Well, we've gone on a great quest in this chapter and hopefully, you've been recharged and motivated to achieve this majestic purpose of unity. Hopefully, you've discovered some of the resources available to you on your journey as well. In review, we've established the quest for humility results in unity, the key of humility removes our vanity, and most importantly the Christ of humility retains all authority. These three Biblical truths are embedded into one of the most treasured passages of Bible, Philippians 2:1-11.

Conclusion

Let me share a true story from a prior generation and a different culture. Even though the culture and the time may be different, the impact and truthfulness of the actions remain transformative.

Watchman Nee was an incredibly brave and courageous Chinese Christian teacher and author of the mid-20th century. He endured great persecution. He was a man who lived his faith and often told a memorable story about a fellow believer in China.

This fellow Christian believer had a rice paddy next to another rice paddy that belonged to a communist official. Every morning the Christian got up and worked a pump that was basically built around a bicycle. (You would pump with your feet, and it would pump water from the river into the rice patty.) Every morning the Chinese Christian pumped that water into his field and as soon as he was finished and left, his communist neighbor came and removed the boards that separated their two rice paddies allowing all of the water to flow into the communist official's rice paddy.

As the believer understood what was going on, he cried out to God. He said, "Lord, I need this rice paddy to provide for my family and if this keeps up, I'm not going to have any rice and we are going to be in absolutely desperate straits." It was at that point in prayer that the Holy Spirit revealed to the believer what to do next.

On the next morning, the Chinese Christian got up earlier than ever, went to the rice paddy and removed the boards, went to the pump, and watered his neighbor's rice paddy. Then he put the boards back in and watered his own. He did that, day after day and in a matter of just a few weeks both rice paddies were flourishing, but something else happened. His communist neighbor became a follower of Jesus because you see, genuine love speaks to even the most hardened of hearts.[56]

Jesus said it this way to His followers in John 13:34, *"A new command I give you: Love one another. As I have loved you, so you must love one another."* The way to love is through servanthood and we do so with humility, just like Jesus did.

You and I can't do this the way we're supposed to on our own. Or in our own power. We have to come to Christ first and humble ourselves at the foot of the cross. But how can we do that if we're separated from God? The Bible tells us that we've all fallen short of God's standard. The Bible also makes it clear that the recompense for our shortfalls is separation from God, both now and for eternity. That's bad news, isn't it? It is. But God didn't want to leave us in that condition, so Jesus came to this planet to redeem us. To set us free from our selfishness and provide a way for us to become the people God designed us to be. People with a purpose. People with a hope. People who love and care for each other. People who know and understand who the true King of Kings and Lord of Lords is. One day you and I will confess Jesus as Lord, either before we pass away or one day in eternity. It's not a matter of if we will confess Him as Lord, but a matter of when. Once we pass through this life, the Bible tells us it's too late. Hebrews 9:27 tells us, *"Each person is destined to die once and after that comes judgment."* Some people think they can get right with God after they die, but this verse clearly says after we pass away judgment awaits. Isn't it better to take care of it now?

Plus, the way to unity is through humility and it's through that humility we find true joy. Isn't that what we're all looking for anyway? Why deprive yourself of God's true joy that's been available this entire time? Furthermore, not only do we find true joy with our Creator, but we also discover true joy with each other.

So, let me ask you, have you humbled yourself before the cross? Have you ever asked Jesus Christ into your heart to be your Lord and Savior? The Bible tells us in Romans 10:9, *"If you openly declare that Jesus is Lord and believe in your heart that God raised him from the dead, you will be saved."* That's the beginning prayer for you and me to start this journey with the Savior. Let me encourage you today, if you haven't already, to say that prayer and invite Jesus Christ into your life. And when you do that, go tell someone about it!

T.K. Anderson

Chapter Six

Rejoice in a Heavenly Citizenship

Philippians 3:1,12-21

We hear a lot about citizenship in almost every election cycle in America. Depending on which side of the political aisle you find yourself, you may be labeled all sorts of things. Concerning the topic citizenship, it doesn't matter if you support legal or illegal immigration, if you say the "incorrect" thing, you'll be instantly roasted and toasted by the opposing party. Sometimes I wonder if all this political banter is just for appearance. The real motive seems to be to create division, anger, and hatred from differing partisan groups in order to win a few votes. I have no idea if it's always been like this in American politics, but something tells me there's *"nothing new under the sun."* (Ecclesiastes 1:9)

Citizenship is a great thing to possess when it's connected to a county that abounds with plentiful resources and vast riches. But no matter the wealth a nation may possess, the benefit of its citizenship is tied to the direction of that nation. Yet, in contrast, the Bible tells us we possess a citizenship that is sealed in heaven and the benefits of this immortal status begin the moment we put our trust in Christ. We can never lose it once we've obtained it. I wonder, though, as born-again believers, how much do we really focus on our heavenly citizenship? It's difficult because we get easily bogged down in the muck and mire of this world. But in reality, this world is nothing more than a train depot where we await the advent of our heavenly departure.

I read a story this week from a pastor who wrote an interesting take on the idea of earth being nothing more than a heavenly gateway. Here's what he wrote, "I recently made a trip to Ellis Island in New York. Ellis Island was once the biggest immigration processing center in the U.S. It processed thousands of immigrants a day. All of these immigrants left their homelands through much difficulty to come to "the land of promise." They believed they could make themselves a new and better life here.

At the time, a trip to America took at least a month by boat. When I went to Ellis Island, I saw dormitory rooms where people stayed while they were being processed. They weren't much to look at from our 21st-century American perspective, but I wonder what they looked like to the 19th-century immigrants. Maybe to some of them, especially after months on a boat, they looked promising. Maybe it was the grandest room they had ever seen. And imagine with me that one person is so overwhelmed with the greatness of this room that he decides he will stay there forever.

And so, when they try to finish processing him, he attempts to stall the process. He hangs up his pictures above the bunk. He unpacks all his clothes and moves right in. You'd want to grab this guy and tell him how foolish he was being. You'd want to explain to him that this place is a dump, and that America has so much more to offer him. And yet, how often do we do the same thing.

Freedom

Surely, this earth is impressive. But it is only the processing center on the way to heaven.[57]

Let me ask you, are you focusing on your citizenship in heaven? In chapter three of his letter to the Philippians Paul changes gears to focus on the ultimate prize awaiting each of us as followers of Christ. And it's something we should really rejoice about. Remember, Philippians is the letter that causes us to rejoice in Christ.

In chapter one, we learned how to rejoice in hardships and how through the difficulties in our life; God allows us to expand the gospel, encourage other believers, exhibit our motives, and equip us for the future. In chapter two, we discovered the example of Christ's humility and how we too can rejoice in emptying ourselves from our cultural self-centeredness as we take on the likeness of our Savior. But here, in chapter three, Paul points out there's a great goal for us to achieve and it will be achieved for all those who put their trust in the saving power of Jesus. He lays out six aspects to our citizenship in heaven. He starts the chapter by saying we should rejoice in the Lord.

Rejoicing in Our Citizenship
"Finally, my brothers, rejoice in the Lord." Philippians 3:1

Like an immigrant standing before a judge as he finally receives his citizenship, we all obtain instant legal standing before God as citizens of heaven at the moment of salvation. It's as if an angel of heaven walks over from the judgment seat of Christ transporting a legal document to the desk of the Holy Spirit who seals the spiritual record with a heavenly mark and then promptly delivers it to the

Father who declares to the realms of heaven and earth, "You are hereby declared a citizen of heaven!" Look how Paul describes this in his letter to the Ephesians, *"For through (Jesus) we both have access in one Spirit to the Father. So, then you are no longer strangers and aliens, but you are fellow citizens with the saints and members of the household of God."* (Ephesians 2:18-19) We are connected to a heavenly home and never to be rejected. Our citizenship is secure, not because of us, but on account of the finished work of Christ.

Because of all this, the command from Paul is for us to rejoice. But rejoice in who you might ask? In the Lord of course, but why should we rejoice? Well, Paul now spends the rest of chapter three laying out for us the reasons for our celebration. In verses two through eleven, Paul describes the incompleteness of relying on good deeds or ceremonies to inherit salvation. Those are the old things required by the law, but we can rejoice because Christ opened the door for us through his finished work on the cross.

We have been freed from the law and its legal demands. This is cause for great joy Paul says. This opening phrase of chapter three is a call to loudly proclaim your happiness. It literally means to loudly exclaim your joy! It carries the idea of rejoicing loudly, as in a trumpeter's hail. When was the last time you exclaimed your joy in that kind of way?

Again, going back to our picture of the courtroom, it's not uncommon for people to let out a yell or a cheer once they've been declared a citizen of our country. Have you done the same thing, or even more, about your heavenly citizenship lately? If not, do it now. Go ahead let out a yell, a hoot, a hail, rejoice! You're a citizen

Freedom

of heaven, never to be lost, taken away, revoked, or declared void.

I remember in high school and college we always invited a really bad team to play against us for homecoming. Did your school do that too? Hopefully, you didn't go to a school that was invited to everyone else's homecoming. But remember those games? We started rejoicing before the game started because we already knew the outcome. As the game progressed, the rejoicing continued. Even if there was a setback, a penalty, or a turnover, it was ok, because we knew we had this. There was no way we would be defeated, not this game, not this night! That's what Paul's trying to get across here, rejoice Philippians, you've got this! He's saying, "Rejoice Christians you've got home-field advantage." He's saying, "We've got way better talent and we've got hyper-intelligent coaching. Plus, we know the One who wrote the rule book."

It sure is good to know the author, isn't it? And it sure is good to know the One who's already written your story too. Did you know the Bible tells us, *"I knew you before I formed you in your mother's womb. Before you were born, I set you apart..."* (Jeremiah 1:5) That's a pretty big statement. The best part is the truth of this verse still applies to you today. God wasn't surprised to hear the news you were on the way. He knew about you before your parents did. As we piece this all together, we're starting to see a pretty cool picture emerge. God knew us and set us apart for His great purpose. It's a purpose with a plan.

Now, when you know you have a reason for being somewhere you often look around for a manual or hand book that kind of provides an outline for you. A sort of sketch for the requirements of your position. I remember one time taking a job as a dishwasher at a very high end and busy restaurant. By the middle of the first night, I was swamped in dirty dishes, pots, pans, and overflowing garbage cans. It was a mess, literally! Sometimes life feels like that doesn't it? But all it takes is someone with some experience to come along side you and slowly and surely get things back on track and moving in the right direction again.

That's what happened for me that night. A co-worker showed up, rolled up his sleeves and we went to work. He used to be the dishwasher, so he knew all the tricks of the trade. In a short time, we were caught up and I learned some valuable lessons that kept me organized in the weeks and months ahead.

In a similar way, that's what Paul is doing for us here in chapter three. He's coming alongside us to give us a little help and encouragement to stay focused, slow down, and not to let the messiness of our situation get us off our game. He moves us forward from simply rejoicing about our citizenship into having a deep desire to live out our divine nationality in a God-honoring way. We may know the outcome, *and rejoice because of it*, yet we still want to play the game right and we want to do the best job we can for the Lord. This thought led Paul to a restlessness for a perfect citizenship. In verse twelve he continues to share his longing to obtain all that God has for him. The second aspect of our heavenly citizenship is connected to the restlessness for a perfect citizenship. Let's see how Paul describes this.

The Restlessness for a Perfect Citizenship

"*[12]Not that I have already obtained this or am already perfect, but I press on to make it my own, because Christ Jesus has made me his own. ¹³Brothers, I do not consider that I have made it my own. But one thing I do: forgetting what lies behind and straining forward to what lies ahead, ¹⁴I press on toward the goal for the prize of the upward call of God in Christ Jesus."* Philippians 3:12-14

There is a story about a great sculptor, who after years of work created a statue so perfectly fashioned that he could discover no line that needed to be corrected, no feature that needed to be remodeled. A friend found the artist in tears. "I shall never do anything better than this," moaned the sculptor. "It is the perfection of my best work."[58] As much as that may be true for the sculptor, there's no need to worry about that type of disappointment in the Christian experience. If you're like me, life teaches us there is always room to grow in Christ.

We find tension in Paul's writing in this set of verses. He knows his future is secure but doesn't want to take it for granted. He doesn't want to put his Christian life on cruise control. Sadly, there are Christians who do that. Perhaps you know of some? Perhaps you have been guilty of doing that at some point too. To avoid this temptation, Paul leaves three clues to aid us in our journey to secure all that God has for us. Those three clues are to forget the past, focus forward, and never quit!

In the middle of verse 13, Paul leaves a very important clue for us. He reminds us that one of the keys to living successfully for God is *"forgetting what lies behind."* It's difficult to follow this advice for many of us. Sometimes it's tough to forget the past. Given the choice, occasionally we're inclined to dwell in the past. When we do, we tend to drag up old memories and recall the former way of life. But Paul reminds us here that doing that works against us. It keeps up bound up to the memory of a thing. Which is odd if we really think about it. Why do we let the shadow of a thing still impact us when the actual thing is long gone? Especially when the actual thing has been forgiven by God a long time ago.

The Bible comes to our rescue on this because if you notice the word choice, Paul uses the present tense verb, "forgetting." Notice he didn't say "I forgot." That would be past tense, as in it's already done. He said, "I'm forgetting." That means it's a process and many times it's a constant process. It's a continual action that we take when old memories come our way. We simply say like Paul, "I'm forgetting what lies behind me." There's a step for us to take in this. We get to do the actual forgetting. God doesn't erase our memories for us, we simply choose to no longer dwell on the things that work against us in our new spiritual life.

When we take this first step of forgetting the past, we can then spend our newly freed energies on being focused forward. Paul's next phrase in the text, *"straining forward to what lies ahead"* is a reminder that the best option in life is to stay determined to look ahead. It's no secret that the windshield of a car is much larger than the review mirror. It's made this way because we need to be looking forward to getting where we want to go. The review mirror is much smaller. It is significant to know where we've come from, but it should not come at the expense of a forward-facing outlook.

The word Paul uses here for *"straining forward"* is *epekteínomai* [ἐπεκτείνομαι]; pronounced ep-ek-ti'-nom-ahee. It means to *stretch (oneself) forward upon:—reach forth.*[59] Interestingly, this is the only place in the Bible this word is used. Again though, just like the first clue, this is a specific action we are to take. Being a citizen of heaven is not a passive thing. It's an active thing. It's about taking a proactive role in making purposeful decisions designed to propel our walk with Christ and our impact for Christ forward. Sometimes that means to really stretch or reach for what God has for us. When was the last time you really reached or stretched out in faith for what God has for you? This is a part of the restlessness for a perfect citizenship.

Once we've forgotten the past and have become focused forward, the third clue Paul leaves us with is to implement the spiritual attitude of never quitting. Notice verse 14, *"I press on toward the goal for the prize of the upward call of God in Christ Jesus."* Pressing on toward the goal is another way to say, I'm not quitting. Winston Churchill once inquired, "Do you know why the nose of the bulldog is sloped backwards? So, it can keep on breathing without ever letting go."[60] There's a tenaciousness that comes with being a heavenly citizen. That's what Paul's getting at here. We don't give up. We don't quit. We press on, toward the goal, for the prize, which is the heavenly call of God found in Christ Jesus.

Vince Lombardi was a world-class coach for the Green Bay Packers and was a winner. He knew a little something about never quitting and once said the following, "Winning is not a sometime thing; it's an all-the-time thing. You don't win once in a while; you don't do things right once in a while; you do them right all of the time. Winning is a habit. Unfortunately, so is losing…Every time a football player goes to practice his profession, he's got to play from the ground up - from the soles of his feet right up to his head. Every inch of him has to play. Some guys play with their heads. That's O.K. You've got to be smart to be number one in any business. But more importantly, you've got to play with your heart, with every fiber of your body. If you're lucky enough to find a guy with a lot of head and a lot of heart, he's never going to come off the field second."[61]

I think that's the type of passion Paul is trying to impart to his friends in Philippi, and by extension, to us as well. He continues on in verse 17 to share with us that we are not without an example. We have representatives of our citizenship to help us along the way.

The Representatives of Our Citizenship

"Brothers, join in imitating me, and keep your eyes on those who walk according to the example you have in us." Philippians 3:17

With two older brothers and an older sister, I was fortunate to be the youngest of four siblings. Some may ask, how is being the youngest a benefit? Let me tell you, because I was the youngest of four, I enjoyed the benefits of seeing what worked right and what to avoid. This benefit was helpful many times. From jumping off our roof and into our pool (*which I don't advise*), to finding out which teacher to take or avoid in junior and senior high school, I held a distinct advantage over some of my closest friends. I also discovered what kind of pranks worked on my parents and which ones didn't. Being the youngest kept me out of a lot of trouble. Yet, truth be told, even though I utilized this benefit many times, sometimes I learned my lessons the hard way just like everyone else. However, the biggest benefit was on the athletic field. I watched, practiced, and put into play many of the things I observed from my older brothers and their friends. And those things I learned; those things really worked. In fact, it worked so well I played way above my natural talent just because I imitated the moves and techniques I learned from those who went before me. It was a huge advantage over those who didn't have had anyone to imitate.

In a similar way, regarding our spiritual life, Paul is saying, *"use us as an example. Don't feel for a moment that you're all alone in your walk with Christ. You've got us as a model."* If fact, Paul is so clear on this point that he actually writes, *"walk according to the example you have in us."* He is very clear on this idea of imitating himself and the other Christian leaders of his day. His main concern rests in the idea that people might be thinking they have to figure out how to follow Jesus all on their own. The beautiful thing about our Christian experience is that it's the exact opposite. We don't have to strive at this all alone. We have wonderful and precious promises from God, and we have wonderful and precious people that have gone before us and travel along with us. People who show us how to persevere and overcome. People who show us how to endure and advance. People who come alongside and teach us to walk in the power and benefit of our heavenly citizenship. Paul is saying find these people and copy them.

He uses two interesting words in verse 17 to drive home this point. The words *"imitate"* and *"example."* These two words provide a phenomenal word picture as it relates to this principle. The word *"imitate"* in the text means to mimic someone. This is such an important concept for Paul that he uses this same phraseology and concept in at least five passages. Twice to the Corinthians, twice to the Philippians, and once in his letter to Titus.

- *"I urge you, then, be <u>imitators</u> of me." 1 Cor 4:16*
- *"Be <u>imitators</u> of me, as I am of Christ." 1 Cor 11:1*
- *"Join in <u>imitating</u> me" Phil 3:17*
- *"What you have <u>learned</u> and <u>received</u> and <u>heard</u> and <u>seen in me</u>—<u>practice these things</u>, and the God of peace will be with you." Phil 4:9*

In these four passages, along with some others, there is a strong emphasis from Paul to inspire his earliest of followers to imitate, or mimic, him in their Christian experience. Paul promises his disciples that as we imitate those who are walking with God, we will begin to experience the presence of God in our life, *"and the God of peace will be with you." (Phil 4:9)* That's pretty amazing, isn't it?

Many people hunger to experience the peace of God in their life and here we have a clear and succinct plan on how to do that. We can find God by imitating the representatives of our citizenship. Yet, there's one more reason behind this strong encouragement. As we dig a little deeper, we find in Paul's personal letter to Titus, a behind the scenes look at why this issue is so important. "Show yourself in all respects to be <u>a model of good works</u>, and in your teaching show integrity, dignity, [8]and sound speech that cannot be condemned, so that an opponent may be put to shame, having nothing evil to say about us." (Titus 2:7-8)

If you know anything about Paul, he was very competitive. He did not like to lose, and he most definitely did not want any of his opponents to gain an upper hand on him or the cause of Christ.

Paul was a disciplined man. He was a straight shooter and very committed to the Lord and the plan God had for his life. Here, he encourages Titus to be *"a model of good works"* so that no one could disqualify him in his teaching about the Lord. When we walk in a way that is representative of our heavenly citizenship it'll stand out. It gives us credibility in our conversations. It goes before us and follows behind us. That's the power of influence in a relationship, in a family, in a workplace, or in a culture. Paul is letting us know we can have this kind of influence.

Here's the really interesting part, this phrase *"a model of good works"* is from the Greek word *typos* τύπος (pronounced too'-pos). It means *'the mark of a stroke or blow, print'* or *'a figure formed by a blow or impression.'* The application is straight forward and it's the same exact word Paul uses in Philippians 3:17, *"walk according to the example you have in us."* The word "example" here is *typos*, the same word we find in Titus 2:7. So, the idea here is to find those in spiritual leadership who exhibit the character qualities of Christ. Follow those who have the image of Christ stamped into and onto their life, and when you find them, follow after them. In turn, you'll be that example to someone else one day.

So, we have representatives of our citizenship, but we must be on guard because in verse eighteen, Paul continues by warning us of…

The Rivals of Our Citizenship

"¹⁸For many, of whom I have often told you and now tell you even with tears, walk as enemies of the cross of Christ. ¹⁹Their end is destruction, their god is their belly, and they glory in their shame, with minds set on earthly things." Philippians 3:18-19

T.K. Anderson

All good stories have a protagonist and an antagonist and our story here on earth is no different. Antagonist is from the Greek language and simply means 'anti' or against and 'agonist' means actor. It's the actor in a story who is against the main character or hero of the story. This is a literary device a writer uses to develop and create a compelling script.

Paul is reminding the Christians in Philippi that there are rivals to our citizenship that attempt to persuade us out of our rights as children of God. They will attempt to deceive us into disavowing our citizenship, or at least the benefits of it. They will add-on religious requirements that are not a part of our heavenly privileges. These are sneaky people, deceptive leaders, misinformed individuals, and quite literally, *"enemies of the cross"* (v 18). Paul calls these people *"dogs"* in verse two and refers to them as *"evil doers"* as well. He really wanted to make a strong point here. Remember, these are the very people that would follow Paul around from town to town the subvert his labors for the Lord by confronting him and even after he left town would stick around and confuse these new believers.

Well, guess what? Things haven't changed much. There are still people in our culture who will confuse you, attempt to deceive you, misinform you, and we need to be on the lookout for anyone, or any organization, that is contrary to the message of the gospel or contradicts the clear teaching found in the Word of God. This is the role of the mature believer in a local body.

One of the primary tasks of a pastor is to look out for false teachings that creep into the body. The picture of a wolf in sheep's clothing is an appropriate analogy for this point. This burden falls to small group leaders, deacons, deaconesses, kids, and teen leaders, as well as worship leaders. These are the people who serve as gate keepers of the gospel against antagonists who want to bring destruction to a healthy body.

How do I spot them, you might ask? They have four characteristics in verse nineteen.

Finality – *"Their end is destruction."* For a Christian, our finality is to glorify Christ, for our rivals they have a different end in mind, and it leads to destruction. Ask them, in your teaching/view, where does this all end?

Food – *"Their god is their belly."* For a Christian, we are called to serve others, pick up our cross daily and other self-limiting disciplines. For these adversaries, they have a different focus to satisfy their individual desires. Their 'food' is to do what makes them full. The Christian's "food" is to do what the Father directs us to.

Fame – *"They glory in their shame."* As Christians, we glory in the name of Christ, the work of Christ, and salvation found in Christ. For these enemies, they find their fame in the very things that are contrary to a mature walk with Christ and in most cases things that are considered dishonoring to the mind of God and anchored in self-promotion.

Framework – *"Minds set on earthly things."* For a Christian, our worldview is set on Scripture and the story of mankind from Creation and the Fall to Redemption, all the way up to the new Heaven and new Earth. For these "dogs" (as Paul called them) have a different worldview that is ultimately not based upon

Scripture. It will always include something different or something more. These are the ones that Paul is telling the Philippians to be on the lookout for. They are rivals to your citizenship and enemies of the cross. They look to pull you down and disrupt what God is doing in your life.

In verse 20, Paul now turns to celebrate again our citizenship and paints a beautiful picture for us of what awaits those who follow Christ. The reality of our citizenship in heaven awaits us.

The Reality of Our Citizenship

" [20]*But our citizenship is in Heaven, and from it we await a Savior, the Lord Jesus Christ,* [21]*who will transform our lowly body to be like his glorious body, by the power that enables him even to subject all things to himself."* Philippians 3:20-21

One of the most amazing aspects of salvation is encapsulated in this idea of receiving a glorified body one day. A body like Jesus had after His physical resurrection from the dead. Some have asked, *what was His body like?* He could eat. He could travel independently of a vehicle. He could walk through objects. He could talk and interact with people. He was recognizable by some yet was able to disguise Himself to others. He ascended into the clouds and will descend to the earth again one day. There's so much more we simply do not understand about this glorified body that is promised to us, but for now we can safely conclude it is somehow not bound by the natural laws of physics we are accustomed to today.

Here's another thing we know, it's a promise from God found

here and in many other passages throughout the Bible and it's one of the direct benefits of salvation. We tend to focus only on forgiveness from sin, deliverance from our old nature, or other elements of salvation. And rightly so, we should focus on those things. But for Paul, this idea of receiving a glorified, or transformed, body one day was also at the forefront of his teaching regarding the blessings and benefits of salvation.

For Paul, when we get saved or get born again, we not only receive forgiveness for all our sins, but we instantly inherit heavenly citizenship. And where is the citizenship secured? In Heaven, that's right. This is a reality as sure as any other reality we interact with every day. Because Christ rose from the dead, as the first fruits of those to follow, we have confidence that He will transform us to be like Himself. That's what this text is saying to us. The word "transform" in the text means, "to change in fashion or appearance." It comes from two words, *meta* meaning "after," implying a change, and *schema*, where we derive our word scheme (meaning system or structure). Putting it all together, "transform" is rendered "He (Christ) shall fashion anew" (our bodies) in the structure following the pattern of His resurrected body.

When will all this happen? It will happen at His return. Elsewhere in the Bible we are told that when Christ returns, He will then transform our physical and deceased bodies into our newly transformed, immortal bodies like His. It's going to be quite a sight to behold during the millennial reign of Christ with hundreds of millions of resurrected saints moving around on planet earth. I say this because this is a reality of our heavenly citizenship. This will happen! We don't talk about it enough, but we should celebrate this reality more frequently.

Sometimes these types of future promises are hard to realize. Because of this, it's easy to set it aside when we can't picture it. But let me share a story with you that may help to understand the simplicity of this great reality.

A woman had been diagnosed with fatal sickness and had been given three months to live. Her doctor told her to start preparing for this new reality. So, she contacted her pastor and had him come to her house to discuss certain aspects of her final wishes. She told him which songs she wanted to be sung at the service, what scriptures she would like to be read, and what she wanted to be wearing. The woman also told her pastor she wanted to be buried with her favorite Bible.

Everything was in order and the pastor was preparing to leave when the woman suddenly remembered something very important to her. "There's one more thing," she said excitedly. "What's that?" came the pastor's reply. "This is very important." The woman continued, "I want to be buried with a fork in my right hand." The pastor stood looking at the woman not knowing quite what to say. "That shocks you, doesn't it?" the woman asked. "Well, to be honest, I'm puzzled by the request," said the pastor.

The woman explained. "In all my years of attending church socials and functions where food was involved, and let's be honest, food is an important part of any church event, spiritual or otherwise, my favorite part was when whoever was clearing away the dishes of the main course would lean over and say 'you can keep your fork.' It was my favorite part because I knew that something better was coming." "When they told me to keep my fork, I knew that something great was about to be given to me. It wasn't Jell-O or pudding, but something really good.

So, I just want people to see me there in that casket with a fork in my hand and I want them to wonder, 'What's with the fork?' Then I want you to tell them, 'Something better is coming, so keep your fork too.'" Paul said that our citizenship is not here on earth, but in heaven above.[62]

A Reflection on Our Citizenship

"[15]Let those of us who are mature think this way, and if in anything you think otherwise, God will reveal that also to you. [16]Only let us hold true to what we have attained." Philippians 3:15-16

Sandwiched in the center of this celebratory and rejoicing passage focused on our citizenship in Heaven, Paul places a logical reflection point in verses 15 and 16. It functions as an intellectual flagpole in the center of this portion of his Philippian text, 3:12-21. We've spent a great amount of time discussing the benefits of our citizenship, our reality, rivals, and representatives, but before we leave this section, we have one more item to consider. That is, how are we to think about all of this? According to Paul, believers who are mature in their faith will reflect upon the truths disclosed to us in this short passage.

Paul does this because we are constantly assaulted from all sides as followers of Christ, our old nature comes against us. The world tries to persuade us. The enemy attempts to lure us. All of this is continual and if we're not careful, we can give in and lose out on what God has for us. One of the ways we can counter these continuous attacks is to get our minds right. Set our thinking right. In other words, get our head screwed on right and keep it there. So much of what we battle isn't out there, it's in here, between our two ears! The battle of the mind isn't won by ignoring it. No, it's won by focusing on those things that help us stay centered on Christ and reflect upon those things that are before us in Him.

Look how Paul describes this for the Corinthians, Ephesians, and Philippians:

- *"Brothers, do not be children in your thinking. Be infants in evil, but in your thinking be **mature**."* (1 Cor 14:20)
- *"Until we all attain to the unity of the faith and of the knowledge of the Son of God, to **mature** manhood, to the measure of the stature of the fullness of Christ."* (Eph 4:13)
- *"Let those of us who are **mature** think this way."* (Phil 3:15)

This wasn't a new idea for Paul. In writing to the Philippians, he utilized this mature thinking concept in the same way as he did with many of his churches throughout the Mediterranean region. Paul knows that the way to enjoy our heavenly citizenship is to reflect upon it often. When was the last time you sat down over a cup of coffee and reflected upon the benefits of your heavenly citizenship? Probably never, right?

Imagine for a moment that you received a passport in the mail. It was a passport with your name and picture on it and it was a passport to Heaven. In the envelope was a ticket, a one-way ticket to Heaven. So, there you have in your hand a ticket and passport to heaven. How would feel at that moment? That's the type of picture we should be reflecting upon more often. Why? Because it's real, that's why. If you're a follower of Jesus Christ, then guess what? You're going to Heaven one day. Your ticket has been purchased and your passport has been created. Have you reflected upon this lately? If not, begin doing so today.

I have to tell you, though, I've been walking with the Lord quite a while now and I know why some of us are hesitant to spend too much time reflecting on our citizenship. We're either ashamed of our past, and somehow don't think we deserve it, or we think we're not going to make it to Heaven because we think we're going to mess up sometime down the road and lose out on all of it.

Well, can I tell you both of those thoughts are not helpful and, frankly, are not biblical. First off, none of us deserve citizenship in Heaven, so let's get that one out of the way. It's given to us by grace because Jesus loves us. Secondly, you're probably right, you are going to mess up sometime in the future, but you're not the one who secures your eternal destination, so you can't lose it. If you've received Christ as your personal Lord and Savior, then the Holy Spirit has sealed you into the family of God. You can't "unseal" it. I hate to break it to you, but you don't have that kind of power.

Let me get a bit more street-level on this issue because it really messes us up. Too many Christians are carrying around a defeated thought process because they aren't living the way they know they should be. I get that. But the solution isn't to give in, the solution is to keep going. Don't give up on what you know God has in store for you. Don't let your failures or mistakes dictate your future. Brush yourself off, come back to Christ and start again. Spiritual success isn't easily earned, it is planned. You have to plan success.

What I mean by that is, know and understand that on this road with Christ, because of the three areas we discussed earlier (us, the world, and our enemy) we will falter and fail from time to time. But knowing that ahead of time, we can also plan on putting our minds right by coming back to Christ. When we plan ahead to deal with our failures, it helps us overcome those mountains of problems, issues, addictions, or destructive habits in our life. Those mountains start to shrink in size when we know we have a way to overcome them. Here's the cool part, the more success we have, the more we don't want to do those old things anymore. We mature past them. That's the message here from Paul. Look, don't allow those negative things to define you any longer. Your identity isn't found in failure, rather it's cultivated by faith. Your identity is found in Christ. Let me share one last story with you that illustrates what I'm trying to say.

In one of the numerous attempts to scale Mount Everest before the final successful attempt in 1953, a group of skilled climbers made a final dash for the summit but failed. Today, those climbers lie buried somewhere beneath the timeless snow. They failed despite their tremendous determination, heroic courage, the discipline of long training, and the personal sacrifice of money and life, to reach the highest point of the highest mountain in the world. When one of the party, having returned to London, was giving a lecture, he had on the platform behind him a magnificent picture of Everest and, as he concluded his address, turned around and speaking as if to the mountain said, "We tried once to conquer you, and failed; we tried again, and you beat us; but we shall yet beat you, for you cannot grow bigger, but we can."[63]

Conclusion

We've gone on a long journey in this chapter taking a robust look at our citizenship in Heaven. We started by looking at how we can best rejoice in what Christ has secured for us. We then considered our desire to press on toward what awaits us. We've surveyed the representatives and rivals of our citizenship as well as the reality of our glorified body at the return of Christ. And lastly, we we're reminded by Paul to reflect upon our citizenship as mature believers are encouraged to do. Which helps us in overcoming our difficulties.

This also brings us to an end of our three-chapter study in the book of Philippians. We began by learning the letter to Philippi is a letter about rejoicing. As we've surveyed three of Paul's most famous passages in this letter, we discovered we can indeed rejoice through hardship, rejoice in humility, all the while rejoicing in our citizenship in Heaven. Paul delivers for us a masterpiece on how to rejoice in all, through all, and ultimately because Christ gave His all.

T.K. Anderson

Interlude between Philippians and Colossians

As the flicker of his candle slowly faded and the chill of another long night brushed across the face of the aging apostle, Paul must have felt a sense of conclusion as the ink dried upon the Philippian parchment. His 2,100-word letter to the Christian believers of Philippi was finished and he rejoiced. After all, the entire letter focused upon this theme of rejoicing so why wouldn't his countenance glint with a sense of joy? The reality of his dark and desolate jail cell was inescapable, yet the focus of his joy was steadfastly on the truths embedded within the newly imprinted text. It's a reminder to us that no matter our circumstances in life we can choose to focus our attention on the truth available outside of our immediate situation. Situations may be good or bad, but God is forever and always good.

Once completed, Paul rolled up and sealed his divinely inspired letter and carefully packed it into the personal belongings of Epaphroditus. The time for his Roman visit to Paul was nearing an end, and Epaphroditus focused anew on his return journey to Philippi. Initially, the bearer of Philippian news to Paul, he was now the bearer of godly encouragement to this important Macedonian town. Epaphroditus must be on his way for the reassuring words must be delivered.

The Bible doesn't tell us how long it was between visitors during the time of Paul's Roman imprisonment. It's possible some of the visitors overlapped and it's just as likely some visitors were months apart. What we do know is at some point a young man named Epaphras was another of Paul's unique guests.

Paul's relationship with Epaphras was first ignited in the city of Ephesus five to ten years earlier. According to Acts 19:10, we read an insightful passage that provides a key to understanding the founding of the church in Colossae. Here's how Luke records it, "This (Paul being in Ephesus) *went on for the next two years, so that people throughout the province of Asia – both Jews and Greeks – heard the word of the Lord."* (Acts 19:10)

We know from the biblical account that Paul influenced many people throughout the region of Ephesus and surrounding cities. Most Bible historians conclude Epaphras came to Ephesus to hear Paul's teaching and brought the Gospel message back to his hometown of Colossae, some 100 miles away. We catch a confirmation of this within the opening portion of the Colossian letter, *"You learned about the Good News from Epaphras, our beloved co-worker. He is Christ's faithful servant, and he is helping us on your behalf."* (Colossians 1:7)

Something happened between the time Epaphras brought the good news of the Gospel to his hometown and the time of his recorded visit to see Paul in Rome. The Gospel, once secure and thriving, was now being tarnished by false teachers with strange and harmful doctrines. Epaphras knew Paul and his love for the Christians of the Lycus Valley. He suspected if he could get to Paul and explain the situation, Paul would provide the necessary advice and direction for the young leader. What Epaphras didn't know was that his thoughtful visit would yield one of history's most spectacular epistles extolling the supremacy of Christ.

Colossae was a small city closely connected to Hierapolis and the more notable city of Laodicea. The church, most likely held in the home of a man named Philemon, was being influenced by a strange mix of outside leaders. The false teachers were teaching a mix of Greek philosophy, mystery religions, and Jewish legalism. As happened in many towns after the early church took hold, false teachers would come into an area with the desire to sway new converts with all sorts of nefarious teachings. Colossae was no exception.

Many themes are covered in Paul's letter, but the main theme centers on the idea of trust. We are free to trust in Christ, that's Paul's main message. Our trust in Christ shouldn't be influenced by those who do not know Him. We shouldn't be persuaded by those who mix the Word of God with strange ideas. We shouldn't be sidetracked by the mysteries embedded within our inability to fully comprehend all things. Paul encourages the Colossians to rely upon Jesus and jettison the empty philosophies, mysterious enigmas, and religious trappings of this world. When we do that, we find tremendous freedom from spiritual bondage.

False teachers are still in our world today. You can mostly spot them by the type of oppression they put people under. If you and I have to do anything to earn God's favor, then we're missing something critical to the idea of divine grace. If you or I have to perform certain tasks, site-specific incantations, or devise cleverly built philosophies, then we're adding something to the perfect sacrifice of Christ upon the cross.

Instead, according to the Bible, we are free to trust in Jesus. We

T.K. Anderson

will discover in this magnificent epistle, the three key principles to help us trust more, all the while avoiding the dangers of spiritual bondage. We find spiritual freedom as we trust in His royalty, trust in His redemption, and trust in His restoration.

Chapter Seven

Trust in His Royalty

Colossians 1:15-20

In his well-known 1978 Harvard address, Soviet dissident, Alexander Solzhenitsyn, began his speech with these impactful words, "Harvard's motto is 'VERITAS.' Many of you have already found out, and others will find out in the course of their lives, that truth eludes us if we do not concentrate our attention totally on its pursuit."[64] Solzhenitsyn was born during a time of great Russian upheaval. A year before his birth, the 1917 Bolshevik Revolution paved the way for the creation of Vladimir Lenin's Soviet Union. Having been born into this newly created communist system, and while serving his country in World War II, Solzhenitsyn understood the capabilities and dangers of totalitarian rule from a personal point of view. Throughout the 1950s and 1960s, he eventually wrote of its dangers and was imprisoned and exiled from his home country for it. Later in life, Solzhenitsyn returned to his Christian faith and remained a staunch critic and important voice of truth until the Soviet Union's final collapse in 1991. He would later return to his homeland to live out his days in peace.

Solzhenitsyn's story is a strong reminder that once truth becomes disoriented in a culture, truth is all but lost. The consequences of this are devastating. Solzhenitsyn argued that the dechristianization of Russian culture was most responsible for the Bolshevik Revolution which ultimately gave rise to global communism. Developing upon this idea, he once stated,

> *"Over a half-century ago, while I was still a child, I recall hearing a number of old people offer the following explanation for the great disasters that had befallen Russia: 'Men have forgotten God; that's why all this has happened. Since then, I have spent well-nigh 50 years working on the history of our revolution; in the process, I have read hundreds of books, collected hundreds of personal testimonies, and have already contributed eight volumes of my own toward the effort of clearing away the rubble left by that upheaval. But if I were asked today to formulate as concisely as possible the main cause of the ruinous revolution that swallowed up some 60 million of our people, I could not put it more accurately than to repeat: 'Men have forgotten God; that's why all this has happened.'"*[65]

Has that happened to you in your personal life? Have you forgotten God during a part of life's journey? Like the people of Russia, was it at that point things began to unravel? If so, you're not alone. It has happened to people, organizations, churches, cultures, and whole countries. When we forget God, we forgo truth. I mentioned this one time on a university campus and one of the educators challenged my reasoning. He questioned me, "Why do you say, 'If we forgo truth, we miss God?'" The simple answer is that truth is not an idea or a concept, but rather, truth is a person. Jesus identified Himself as such, *"I am the way, and <u>the truth</u>, and the life. No one comes to the Father except through me."* (John 14:6) Therefore, when we forget God, by the nature of His being, we forgo truth.

Freedom

The reason truth is in such limited supply right now is that without Christ, *"our truth"* becomes nothing more than a subjective worldview or personal belief. The secularist is right in defending his idea of *"your truth"* and *"my truth"* in that way. But his thinking is flawed because, in reality, it's not truth, which is yours or mine to have, unless the truth we're referring to is the Lord Jesus Christ and His teachings as found throughout the Bible. The written Word is the living Word concealed, while the living Word is the written Word revealed.

This idea of finding truth was the exact struggle taking place in the city of Colossae during the time of Paul. It was a time in which a plethora of gods, goddesses, spirit beings, ideologies, and philosophies were thrust upon this Greco-Roman culture. Colossae was a town stirring with idol worship, pagan gods, mysticism, and the beginning stages of Gnosticism. These new followers of Christ were being led astray by false teachers who were convincing, charismatic, and cryptic. As Epaphras shares the challenging news with Paul, he knows instantly a letter needs to be sent, to set their hearts and minds at ease. A letter detailing whom we can trust when everything around us is cracked, confusing, and contradictory. A letter that is useful to give a clear passage through a sea of ideological and spiritual uncertainty. A letter that ultimately applies to our culture today and gives us clear direction in our personal life.

In this beautiful letter, Paul is saying to them, and now to us, in a world that is untrustworthy, we can trust in the royalty of Christ. In the passage before us, Colossians 1:15-20, Paul lays out six features describing the divinity of Christ and His royal ancestry based exclusively upon one of the early hymns of the church. The lesson for us here is that Christ's Divine Kingdom is greater than all the kingdoms of this world and He reigns supreme above it all. We start with the first truth that Jesus Christ is the icon of God.

He is the Icon of God

"He (Jesus) is the image of the invisible God." Colossians 1:15a

There is a famous story by Mark Twain called, *The Prince and the Pauper.* In this story, a prince invites a poor beggar into his castle, and for fun, the two exchange clothes. As the story goes, the beggar, being mistaken for the prince, is kept in the castle and lives the life of a prince. But unfortunately, the prince is mistaken for the beggar and is thrown out of the castle. Now, had the prince known that he would be thrown out of the castle, I'm sure he never would have agreed to change clothes with the beggar. Dabbling in such simple fun could never be worth losing so much.

In some ways, the situation in Colossae during the first century resembled the story of The Prince and the Pauper. The Christians in Colossae were being tempted to exchange the great privileges in Christ for the practice of pagan forms of worship. So, Paul shares an early hymn of the Church to remind the Colossians of the tremendous riches and royal privileges we enjoy in Christ, and to warn them of the serious consequences of trading these blessings for the meager benefits that idolatry pretended to offer.[66]

For thousands of years before Jesus, nobody had ever seen God. God had revealed Himself in other ways for certain, but to actually see Him, talk to Him, or touch Him, was not something they were expecting to do. But when Jesus arrived on the scene, something changed all that. People actually interacted with God in a one-on-one format. They ate with God, spoke with God, sailed with God, laughed with God, and even cried with God; it must have been spectacular. He wasn't "like" God. He wasn't an ambassador for God. He wasn't a representative on behalf of God. He was much more than that. Paul is saying here Jesus is God, *"He is the image of the invisible God"* Colossians 1:15a. The opening line of verse 15 sets Jesus apart from the other statue deities and spiritual symbols the Colossians were accustomed to. Those were mere sculptures, poems, or stories of folklore. The contrast is not to be missed here.

In the original language, Paul uses the word "eikon," pronounced (i-kone) for the word we translate as image. This is the same root word we also develop the word icon from. What this means is that God is no longer a mystery. We finally have a chance to see Him. We don't have to look at a statue, a picture, or a fictitious rendering. Those would be graven images anyway and we already know from the Ten Commandments that God speaks against that form of idolatry and worship. Yet, In Christ, we finally have the image of God in the flesh. We need icons, don't we? Icons help us to remember and recall the truth of what it represents.

According to a recent NY Post article, new research shows the simple apple logo of the tech giant bearing the same name has been chosen as the most recognizable logo in the United States. This same study of 2,000 Americans also showed the yellow "M" symbol of McDonald's and the Coca-Cola logo among the most well-known. Nike, Starbucks, and Google all made the top ten with Facebook, Adidas, Amazon, and YouTube rounding out the list. More than a third of those polled (36%) say the logo itself helps them remember a brand.[67]

T.K. Anderson

There's an interesting exchange in Matthew chapter 22 between Jesus and a group of religious leaders. They essentially attempt to trick Jesus through a conversation about paying taxes to Caesar. Nobody likes to pay taxes, right? The people of the ancient world were no different from us. Jesus, knowing what they're up to asks them to get a coin and then asks one of the most impactful questions throughout the entire Bible. They hand Him a coin and Jesus holds it up and asks, *"Whose image is this?"* (Matthew 22:20) In another translation, He continues by saying, *"Whose picture and title are stamped on it?"* You most likely know the rest of the story. They respond, "Caesar," and Jesus tells them, well then, *"Give to Caesar what belongs to Caesar, and give to God what belongs to God."* (Matthew 22:21) I often have thought this would have been a perfect time for Jesus to say, "Whose image is stamped on your soul?" Well, if you know your Bible, Jesus didn't ask that, but let me ask you that today, who's image is stamped upon your soul? If it's God, then give to God what belongs to God!

You see in times of darkness, in times of discontent, in times of cultural unease and shadowy truths. We, as children of God, can look inside, deep into our souls, and know we have the image of God stamped upon our hearts. Just as much as those coins with the image of Caesar belonged to Caesar, how much more, do we who have accepted Christ belong to Him.

Knowing that Christ is the image of God helps me when I pray when I'm putting the pieces of life's puzzle together, or when I need to know what to do. What would Jesus do (WWJD) becomes more than a slogan, it becomes a real question that we can ask and answer in everyday situations. The second quality of Christ we find is that Christ is the imminent authority throughout creation.

Freedom

He is the Imminent Authority Throughout Creation

"The firstborn of all creation." Colossians 1:15b

The world talks a lot about authority, doesn't it? We ask questions like; who has it, how do I get it, or are those in authority abusing it? This whole idea about authority reminds me of a story I heard about an old rancher in the State of Texas. A Drug Enforcement officer stopped by a ranch and spoke with an old rancher. He told the rancher, "I need to inspect your ranch for illegally grown drugs." The rancher said, "Okay, but do not go in that field over there," as he pointed out the location.

The DEA officer verbally exploded saying, "Mister, I have the authority of the Federal Government with me." Reaching into his rear pants pocket, he removed his badge and proudly displayed it to the rancher. "See this badge? This badge means I am allowed to go wherever I wish...on any land. No questions asked or answer given. Have I made myself clear? Do you understand?"

The rancher nodded politely, apologized, and went about his chores. A short time later, the old rancher heard loud screams and saw the DEA officer running for his life being chased by the rancher's big 2,000-pound bull. With every step, the bull gained ground on the officer, and it started looking like he might get gored before he reached safety. The officer was clearly terrified. The rancher threw down his tools, ran to the fence, and yelled at the top of his lungs, "Your badge, officer! Show him your BADGE!"

There's a funny thing about authority, most everybody wants it, and when we have it, we're tempted to display it. But the reality is, if you have authority without the wisdom to handle it, it often ends in a catastrophe. And when it comes to knowing and exercising the truth, the one with authority should be the one who is the most trustworthy. I think that's what Paul is getting at here in this second point found in the text. Jesus is *"the firstborn of all creation."* This means He has imminent authority over everything we could ever possibly see, hear, or interact with within this life and in the life to come.

But some have asked, what does this phrase *"firstborn"* mean? Does this mean that Jesus was created at some point in the past? Was Jesus born like we are? This was a big debate in the fourth century between two guys named Arius and Athanasius. Arius claimed there was a time when Jesus was not. Thereby teaching that Jesus was not the same as the Father or Holy Spirit. But Arius was wrong and in large part, Athanasius used this verse in Colossians 1:15 & 17 as some of his proof texts. Eventually, Arianism was condemned as heresy at the Council of Nicaea in 325 A.D., and his teaching was finally put to rest some 60 years later at the First Council of Constantinople in 381 A.D.

"Firstborn" in this context means to be first in station and authority, not in physicality. The firstborn doesn't have to be the first child born. For example, a firstborn male could be younger than his sisters, or a third brother could be declared the firstborn if the older brothers were removed.

What the Bible is teaching us here is that Christ has all the authority of a firstborn from the Father. That means when we go to the Father and pray in Jesus' name we are going under His authority over all creation. That's why we declare in the name of

Jesus when we wage spiritual warfare. Let me share some passages from the early Church found in the book of Acts and how they would pray or teach in the name of Jesus. These early Christians knew and understood this principle extremely well.

For Baptism into the Body of Christ
"Repent and be baptized every one of you in the name of Jesus Christ for the forgiveness of your sins, and you will receive the gift of the Holy Spirit." (Acts 2:38)

For the Healing of our Infirmities
"I have no silver and gold, but what I do have I give to you. In the name of Jesus Christ of Nazareth, rise up and walk!" (Acts 3:6)

For the Salvation of our Souls
"And there is salvation in no one else, for there is no other name under Heaven given among men by which we must be saved." (Acts 4:12)

For Deliverance from our Enemy
"Paul, having become greatly annoyed, turned and said to the spirit, 'I command you in the name of Jesus Christ to come out of her.' And it came out that very hour." (Acts 16:18)

What's going on here? In all these examples what we see is that all creation answers to Jesus because ultimately, He has authority over all of it. This is a great encouragement to us because as we go through situations that seem to be overpowering for us, we know that we can go to the One who has the power over all of it. Jesus is the One who can deliver us, save us, restore us, or revive us. He is the ultimate authority in this world, and we can trust He knows how to use His authority wisely in our life. Next, let's look at the third element of Christ's nature that helps us to trust in His royalty.

He is the Instrument of Life

"For by him all things were created, in Heaven and on earth, visible and invisible, whether thrones or dominions or rulers or authorities—all things were created through him and for him." Colossians 1:16

There are a lot of discussions these days on the origin of life. Who should get the credit for it? God or chance? Where did we come from? How did it all begin? I mean if we are indeed just a product of time plus matter, plus chance, then I guess everything we conclude about life, meaning, and purpose is all for nothing. It's every man for himself. But if the Bible is correct in Genesis 1:1, *"In the beginning God created the heavens and the earth,"* that means God has a say in my life and how I should live it, enjoy it, and how I can be in eternity with Him one day. But some say, wait a minute, believing in God is like believing in something you can see, right? That reminds me of a story I heard about a junior high school teacher telling her class about evolution and how the way everything in the world was formed proved that God doesn't exist. She said, "Look out the window. You can't see God, can you?" The kids shook their heads. "Look around you in this room. You can't see God, can you?" The kids shook their heads. "Then our logical conclusion is that God doesn't exist, does He?" she asked at last, certain that she had won her audience over.

But one girl from the back of the classroom said, "Miss Smith, just because we can't see it doesn't mean it doesn't exist. We could do brain surgery and investigate the parts of your brain and we could do a CAT scan and see the brain patterns in your head. But we couldn't prove that you've had a single thought today. Does that mean that you haven't thought anything today? Just because you can't see it doesn't mean it doesn't exist."

In the text here, Paul is confronting a very real worldview of the Greco-Roman period. These were people who often attributed creative powers to angelic beings, elements and/or astral powers. Paul was putting that philosophy to rest by declaring there is only one instrument of life in the universe and that is Jesus Christ. We're not the first culture to wrestle with this issue, nor will we be the last. But the Bible is abundantly clear that Jesus is the creator of all things, and all these things were created for Him too.

Have you ever thought about that before? You were created by Jesus, and you were created for Him too. Wow, that's pretty cool, isn't it? You're not a mistake, you're not a mishap, you're not an afterthought or an oops! According to the Bible, all life is created by Him, and for Him. That means I was created by Him and for Him. You and I are a part of the "All Things" In this text. Let's put our theory to the test...

"All things were created, in heaven and on earth, visible and invisible." I'm a thing, I'm located on the earth, and I'm a visible being, therefore I qualify in this verse. And so do you! That's powerful – You and I are created by Christ Himself!

What does that mean? That means I don't have to worry about anything visible or invisible, or any dominion, ruler, or authority doing anything to me or against me that does not move through the hand of God first. Everything is subject to His sovereignty and divine authority. That's what Paul is getting at here and that's why we can trust Him.

T.H. Huxley, who was called "Darwin's Bulldog," was an English biologist, anthropologist, and advocate of the theory of evolution. He was also a well-known agnostic. He was with a group of men at a weekend house party. On Sunday morning, while most of them were preparing to go to church, he approached a man known for his Christian character and said, "Suppose you stay at home and tell me why you are a Christian." The man, knowing he couldn't match wits with Huxley, hesitated. But the agnostic said gently, "I don't want to argue with you. I just want you to tell me simply what this Christ means to you." The man did, and when he finished, there were tears in Huxley's eyes as he said, "I would give my right hand if only I could believe that!"

Friend, can I tell you this is a story of a man who's being honest, and in a moment of clarity, he instinctively knew the message of this verse. Christ is the creator of life, and we owe every breath to Him. If you know Christ, it's a story like this that causes you to be thankful for the grace of God in Christ that He saw it fit to reveal Himself to you. And if you do not know Christ, this story reminds us that faith in Christ is not done by mental assent alone. The next element of Christ's character found in this early hymn of the church is that He is the irrefutable Lord.

He is the Irrefutable Lord

"And he is the head of the body, the church." Colossians 1:18a

There are a lot of things we can argue about. Some are important, but most are rather trivial. A mother was preparing

Freedom

pancakes for her sons, Kevin, 5, and Ryan, 3. The boys began to argue over who would get the first pancake. Their mother saw the opportunity for a moral lesson. "If Jesus were sitting here, He would say, 'Let my brother have the first pancake, I can wait.'"

Kevin turned to his younger brother and said, "Ryan, you be Jesus!"

You know, it's one thing to argue over a batch of pancakes, but it's a whole other thing to argue over who has control over your life, isn't it? In the city of Colossae, Paul was dealing with false teachers that were placing systems, structures, or secret knowledge above Christ as the head of the Church. Well, according to this little verse in this first-century hymn, there's only one boss of this show and His name is Jesus. Sometimes it's important for us to remember that Christ is the head of the Church. He's the one who's in control. We get into way too many church scuffles trying to assert who's in charge, don't we? We say things like, "That's my committee," "That's my department," or, That's my ministry." And if we're not careful, we begin to act as if we're the one in charge and not Jesus. So many church battles could be avoided by simply remembering whose Church it is. It all belongs to Him, and we are just caretakers for a short period of time.

We tend to do the same in our personal lives, don't we? We think things like, that's my movie night, those are my personal funds, or that's just the way I say things. Be careful, because if Jesus is the Lord of the Church and you're a member of His Body, then that means He's the Lord of your life too!

During the time of Jesus, and up until a few generations ago, most people would have had a good understanding of what "Lord" meant. Yet in our world, sometimes we struggle with it. We don't quite get it. The servant-lord relationship was one of authority and ultimate sovereignty. The lord of the castle, or lord of the land owned it all and he was the one who decided what happened in his modest kingdom. Now take that picture and expand it out to include the entire world, solar system, galaxy, and universe. In fact, think of all of creation, everything seen and unseen, for all time and eternity, it's all His, it all belongs to Jesus. He is the King of Kings and Lord of Lords. And we serve Him. But some may ask, what difference does it make if you serve Jesus, if you make Him your Lord?

In his best-selling book, *A Shepherd Looks at Psalm 23,* Christian author, Phillip Keller, writes, "As I have moved among men and women from all strata of society as both a lay pastor and as a scientist, I have become increasingly aware of one thing. It is the boss, the manager, the master in people's lives who makes the difference in their destiny.

I have known some of the wealthiest men on this continent intimately—also some of the leading scientists and professional people. Despite their dazzling outward show of success, despite their affluence and their prestige, they remained poor in spirit, shriveled in soul, and unhappy in life. They were joyless people held in the iron grip and heartless ownership of the wrong master.

By way of contrast, I have numerous friends among relatively poor people—people who have known hardship, disaster, and the struggle to stay afloat financially. But because they belong to Christ and have recognized Him as Lord and Master of their lives, their owner and manager, they are permeated by a deep, quiet, settled peace that is beautiful to behold.

It is indeed a delight to visit some of these humble homes where men and women are rich in spirit, generous in heart, and large of soul. They radiate a serene confidence and quiet joy that surmounts all the tragedies of their time.

They are under God's care, and they know it. They have entrusted themselves to Christ's control and found contentment.

In another portion of Paul's writings, he provides a wonderful description of this whole discussion by telling us at the end of it all we will all come to the place of recognizing Jesus as Lord. Here's what the Bible tells us in Philippians 2,

"9Therefore God exalted him (Jesus) to the highest place and gave him the name that is above every name, 10that at the name of Jesus every knee should bow, in heaven and on earth and under the earth, 11and every tongue acknowledge that Jesus Christ is Lord, to the glory of God the Father." (Philippians 2:9-11)

Someone once said, "You will acknowledge Jesus as Lord. It's not a matter of *if* but a matter of when." The interesting part is that when we come to Him on this side of eternity, the Bible tells us we secure our place in Heaven with Him. If we wait until after we die, the Bible tells us it's too late and we will spend eternity apart from Christ and His kingdom. Let me encourage you, don't wait!

Let's take a look at the fifth part of the character of Christ that helps us put our complete trust in Him and not in the kingdoms of this world.

T.K. Anderson

He is the Incarnation of the Godhead

"For in him all the fullness of God was pleased to dwell." Colossians 1:19

A pastor friend of mine once wrote, "At the end of the Old Testament era, God the Father did something unheard of: He sent the second Person of the Trinity to become a man and dwell among us."

Someone once said, "Jesus was the way that God sent His 'idea' to humanity; there was and is no better way!" Ignatius, one of the early church fathers, explained that "by the Incarnation, God broke His silence." Less scholarly as an explanation, but equally to the point, was the remark of a little girl who said, "Some people couldn't hear God's inside whisper and so He sent Jesus to tell them out loud."

"The fullness of God," Paul wrote. But if you recall this phrase wasn't something revealed to Paul first. This was a revealed truth given to the early Church and they codified this into one of their early hymns. This is foundational thinking for the early Church. This is bedrock faith for Christians. But what does it mean?

Perhaps an illustration can help us along? There is a painting in a famed palace in Rome by the artist Guido Reni. It is painted into the ceiling of the dome, over 100 feet high. If you were to stand at floor level and look upward, the painting would seem to be surrounded by a fog that leaves its content unclear to those below. However, in the center of the great dome room is a huge mirror, which in its reflection picks up the picture. By looking into the mirror, you can see the picture with great clarity. Comparably, Jesus Christ, born in a manger at Bethlehem, is the mirror of God. In Him, we see a clear reflection of the Father. Jesus said, "If you have seen me, you have seen the Father."

Paul was saying to the false teachers of Colossae, who were worshipping lesser deities and irrelevant spiritual beings, that it was only Christ in which the fullness of God dwelled. The Supreme Creator of the world dwelt in human form in all His fullness in the person of Jesus. But again, some have asked, why did He do this? Why did God come to earth and dwell among us? The insightful Renaissance thinker, Martin Luther, articulates it best by writing, "I would not have you contemplate the deity of Christ, the majesty of Christ, but rather his flesh. Look upon the Baby Jesus. Divinity may terrify man. Inexpressible majesty will crush him. That is why Christ took on our humanity, save for sin, that he should not terrify us, but rather that with love and favor He should console and confirm."

Luther hits the nail on the head. Because God became flesh, we can connect with Him on a personal level. We can relate to God because we know He can understand what we're going through. The writer of Hebrews said it this way, *"(Jesus) understands our weaknesses, for he faced all of the same testings we do, yet he did not sin"* Hebrews 4:15. That means God understands what I'm going through.

You see, we don't serve a God who is far off. A God that is unconnected to our reality. A God who doesn't know what it's like to take a loss, face betrayal, or be lied about. Jesus faced all these things and more, and yet the Bible is clear in telling us that He didn't sin. He got through it all. He conquered life. That means He knows the way out. He knows the way of escape. As we follow Him, we can trust in His power to help us along the way too.

There's a second thing that happens because of the Incarnation of Jesus and I don't want you to miss it. It means that His sacrifice is valid. The Bible tells us, *"According to the law of Moses ... without the shedding of blood, there is no forgiveness."* (Hebrews 9:22) We know that to mean the same thing as we find in Romans 6:23, *"for the wages of sin is death."* So, this means the only way for us to pay the penalty for our sinful actions is to one day die and be separated from God. But in Christ, we have a great redemption. And it's precisely because He took on human flesh that Jesus can become our substitute.

It was His vicarious substitutionary atonement upon the cross that satisfies the penalty we owe to God because of our actions. It was His humanness that makes it actionable. I can't die for your sin. You can't die for my sin. Only a perfect sinless person can do that. When you place your trust in Him, this allows you to join Jesus in Heaven one day. In fact, the Bible circles back on this whole discussion by teaching us, *"With his own blood— (Jesus) entered the Most Holy Place once for all time and secured our redemption forever."* (Hebrews 9:12)

Let's take a look at the sixth and final quality of Jesus that allows us to trust in His royalty above all the kingdoms and ideologies of this world.

He is the Intermediary between God and Man

"And through him to reconcile to himself all things, whether on

earth or in heaven, making peace by the blood of his cross." Colossians 1:20

One of the things I've learned in life is that we're pretty good at pretending to be something we're not, especially when we can benefit from it. Isn't that true? We've mastered the ability to become chameleons, charlatans, or counterfeits, haven't we? I mean not all the time, but there are times when we put on the appropriate face or adjust our appearance and behavior to either fit in, cash in, or influence others to get what we want.

The creator of the famous fictitious detective Sherlock Holmes was a man named Sir Arthur Conan Doyle. One day, Doyle was waiting for a taxi outside the railway station in Paris. An accommodating taxi driver drove up, put Doyle's suitcase in, and got in himself. As Doyle was about to tell the taxi driver where to go the driver said, "Where can I take you, Mr. Doyle?" Doyle was astounded. He asked the driver if he recognized him by sight. The driver said, "No sir, I have never seen you."

Puzzled, Doyle asked how the driver knew he was Conan Doyle. The driver responded, "This morning's paper had a story that you were on vacation in Marseilles. This is the taxi stand where people who return from Marseilles always wait. Your skin color tells me you were on vacation. The ink spot on your right index finger suggests to me that you are a writer. Your clothing is English, not French. Adding up all those pieces of information, I deduce that you are Sir Arthur Conan Doyle."

Doyle exclaimed, "This is truly amazing. You are a real-life counterpart to my fictional character, Sherlock Holmes." "There is one other thing," the driver said. "What's that?" Doyle asked. "Your name," said the driver "is printed on the front of your suitcase."

Isn't it refreshing when we come clean and recognize who we really are? If we could only lose the front more often and be transparent with who we really are. This last portion of this early hymn in verse 20 connects us to the reality of who Jesus is. Although we can fake it till we make it, Jesus isn't like that. He doesn't have to fake anything. We learn here in verse 20 that Jesus is the true reconciler.

In fact, He's the only reconciler between us and the Father. The unique difference between Jesus and all religious systems could not be clearer. All religious systems are attempts of man to earn favor or merit with God. It's our way to climb up the ladder to God. Only in Christ are we saying that it is God who climbed down to us. He is our Creator who came to His creation. It is God, in Christ, who provides salvation. There is nothing more for us to do because everything has already been done.

So, what does it mean to be reconciled to God through Christ? It means I can relax and slow down, my worry can be left at the door. Jesus has this! It means I have a Divine Counsel in Heaven one day. *"He's with me,"* Jesus will say to the Father, *"Put his deeds on my account."* It means my identity is found in Him. I don't have to create one, manufacture one, uphold one, manage one, or constantly reinvent myself for others. I am who He made me to be. I can be settled in who I am. I can stop pretending to be someone that I'm not and start depending on His grace to see me through.

Conclusion

In this chapter we've looked at six qualities of Jesus that allow us to place our trust in Him. These six qualities of Christ are far superior to anything this world has to offer. We learned first that it is through Jesus we can know who God is because He is the Image of God. Next, we learned that Jesus is the firstborn over all creation which means He has imminent authority over everything we could ever possibly see, hear, or interact with in this life and in the life to come. Next, we discovered that Jesus is the agent of Creation. You're not a mistake, you're not a mishap, you're not an afterthought or an oops! According to the Bible, all life is created by Him, and for Him. Following this, we noticed that Jesus is the irrefutable Lord. And we uncovered from Philippians 2 that, *"At the name of Jesus every knee should bow ... and every tongue confess that Jesus Christ is Lord."* One day, every person will confess Him as Lord. Then we discovered that Jesus is God incarnate. He became one of us so that He could qualify as our substitute on the cross. Lastly, we learned that Jesus is the true reconciler between us and our Heavenly Father. It is through Christ that I can be who I truly am and can stop pretending and stop attempting to be good enough on my own.

All of these six qualities of Jesus are found within this early hymn of the church as Paul embedded this hymn for us in Colossians 1:15-20. But this hymn, this passage of Scripture, the power of these truths won't impact your life until you open your heart to receive it. Have you done that yet?

In 1992, the Washington Redskins won the Super Bowl with an explosive victory over the Buffalo Bills. Seventy-five thousand people gathered on the mall between the Capitol and the Washington Monument to cheer their team and Coach. Four days later, Chuck Colson called the Redskins' office to see if any football players could attend a rally at a prison the next day. Many of the players had given their life to Christ. Joe Gibbs, the head coach, answered the phone and told Colson that all the players had left the city for a well-deserved rest. With his characteristic humility, Joe Gibbs asked Colson, "Will I do?"

Colson immediately accepted the offer by the coach of the championship Washington Redskins. Five days after winning the Super Bowl, Joe Gibbs could have opened any door in Washington DC, but he was willing to walk behind the locked steel doors of the penitentiary for the District of Columbia to speak to men about his faith in Christ.

Joe Gibbs stood up to speak to the cheers, whistles, and applause of 500 prisoners five days after he had won the most prestigious event in pro sports. He told those men:

"A lot of people in the world would probably look at me and say: Man, if I could just coach in the Super Bowl, I'd be happy and fulfilled... But I'm here to tell you, that it takes something else in your life besides money, position, football, power, and fame. The vacuum in each of our lives can only be filled through a personal relationship with our Lord and Savior Jesus Christ. Otherwise, I'm telling you, we'll spend the rest of our lives in a meaningless existence. I've seen it in football players' eyes, and I've seen it in men who are on their deathbeds. There's nothing else that will fill the vacuum."

Those are wise words from coach Gibbs. Many people spend

their entire lives searching, hoping, and longing for peace and love. While they search the world and come up empty-handed and wounded-hearted Jesus is standing with arms open, ready to receive them. Don't wait another day. Don't wait another moment. Come to Christ in humility of heart and bow the knee of your heart to the Lordship of Jesus Christ and allow His sacrifice upon the cross to reconcile you back to your heavenly Father.

T.K. Anderson

Chapter Eight

Trust in His Redemption

Colossians 2:6-15

Trust is a peculiar thing. It can take a lifetime to build and yet can be easily lost in a moment. Many times we are prone to trust too easily, especially if it is something or someone we really like. While other times we withhold trust for reasons hard to define. When we don't know what to do, we often look to experts to provide us with trustworthy information so we can make better decisions. But that too has its flaws because many times even the experts prove to be untrustworthy. For example, here are some predictions for the future. All from people who could be trusted:

"While theoretically and technically possible, television may be feasible, yet commercially and financially it is an impossibility." Lee de Forest, inventor.

"The concept is interesting and well-formed, but to earn better than a 'C,' the idea must be feasible." A Yale University management professor in response to Fred Smith's paper proposing reliable overnight delivery service. (Smith went on to found Federal Express Corporation)

T.K. Anderson

"Radio has no future. Heavier-than-air flying machines are impossible. X-rays will prove to be a hoax." William Thomson, Lord Kelvin, British scientist, 1899.

"There is no reason anyone would want a computer in their home." Ken Olson, President, Chairman, and Founder of Digital Equipment Corporation., 1977.

"With over 50 foreign cars already on sale here, the Japanese auto industry isn't likely to carve out a big slice of the U.S. market." Business Week, August 2, 1968.

"Stocks have reached what looks like a permanently high plateau." Irving Fisher, Professor of Economics, Yale University, 1929.

"There is not the slightest indication that nuclear energy will ever be obtainable. It would mean that the atom would have to be shattered at will." Albert Einstein, 1932.

"There will never be a bigger plane built." A Boeing engineer, after the first flight of the 247, a twin-engine plane that holds ten people.

All this back-and-forth of information, ideas, and instructions can cause us to be frozen in our ability to make clear-headed decisions. So, what are we to do? Who are we to trust? It's one thing to have a lack of trust as it relates to everyday decisions, whether big or small, but honestly speaking we can most likely get along just fine. But it's quite another thing to have a lack of trust as it relates to our spiritual life, especially in connection with our eternal salvation. This is one area where we most definitely want to know whom to trust.

Freedom

Thinking back to Paul's letter to the Colossians, soon after Paul left the city of Colossae, we remember that these new followers of Jesus were being influenced by false teachers. Teachers who followed Paul and were determined to win over the new converts to their line of deceptive teaching. When he heard the news of this, Paul expressed his heart for the believers in Colossae by writing, *"For I want you to know <u>how great a struggle I have for you</u> and for those at Laodicea and for all who have not seen me face to face."* (Colossian 2:1)

Here we see the apostle's wonderful pastoral heart for his people. Paul knows and understands the critical nature of this letter especially as it relates to redemption. Spiritual gurus, both now and throughout history, have always attempted to confuse the simple message of the gospel for their own benefit. Paul's big goal in chapter two of his letter is to make the unequivocal case that we can trust in Christ, and Christ alone, for our redemption.

Interestingly, the apostle lays the foundation of chapter two a few verses earlier by writing, *"He has <u>delivered</u> us from the domain of darkness and <u>transferred</u> us to the kingdom of his beloved Son, ¹⁴ in whom we have <u>redemption,</u> the <u>forgiveness</u> of sins."* (Colossians 1:13-14) Paul wants his readers to know there is nothing apart from the person of Jesus Christ that can save us. Jesus is the only one qualified, glorified, and magnified to deliver, transfer, forgive, and redeem us from the domain of darkness and the curse of sin.

It's a redemption that is sweeping. Not only do we owe our existence to our Creator, but we owe our redemption to Him as well. It's a double, all-inclusive program in which we are twice rescued. And Paul wants his readers to grasp this all-important truth.

A gathering of friends at an English estate nearly turned to tragedy when one of the children strayed into deep water. The gardener heard the cries for help, plunged in, and rescued the drowning child. That youngster's name was Winston Churchill. His grateful parents asked the gardener what they could do to reward him. He hesitated, then said, "I wish my son could go to college someday and become a doctor." "We'll see to it," Churchill's parents promised.

Years later, while Sir Winston was prime minister of England, he was stricken with pneumonia. The country's best physician was summoned. His name was Dr. Alexander Fleming, the man who discovered and developed penicillin. He was also the son of that gardener who had saved young Winston from drowning. Later Churchill remarked, "Rarely has one man owed his life twice to the same person."[68]

For those who know this beautiful redemption, Churchill's story is their story too. We come to know that we indeed owe our life twice to our Savior, Jesus. That beauty, that amazement, that wonder should never be lost, taken, or given away. That is precisely Paul's heart as he wonderfully describes four qualities of our redemption through Christ in chapter two verses 6-15.

Let's look at the first trustworthy quality of our redemption.

A Redemption that is Comprehensive

"*6Therefore, <u>as you received</u> Christ Jesus the Lord, so <u>walk</u> in* him, ⁷<u>rooted</u> and <u>built up</u> in him and <u>established</u> in the faith, just as you were taught, <u>abounding</u> in thanksgiving." Colossians 2:6-7*

One of the questions you will be asked when buying new auto insurance is, "Would you like comprehensive coverage on your policy?" For your next vacation, you may find that many beautiful resorts and vacation destinations offer an all-inclusive package. We understand the meaning of these terms. It means that everything is covered. It means there is nothing more to ask for, there is nothing more to add on, and there is nothing more to consider. Similarly, our redemption is comprehensive in three specific ways. Let's dive into verse six.

In its Reach

"Therefore, <u>as you received</u> Christ Jesus the Lord." v 6

First, we notice that our redemption is comprehensive in its reach. One of the most amazing things about the love of God and our redemption is that it is for everyone. No one is excluded from God's grace. Notice that Paul writes, "as **you** received Christ Jesus," he doesn't restrict the audience. He doesn't limit who's allowed, so to speak. There are no limits to who is a qualified candidate to receive the offer of salvation. Using "you" is perhaps the most generic way to include everybody within a population. "Hey, you!" Well, that could apply to anyone, right? Imagine yelling the phrase "Hey, you!" in a sports arena full of people, how many would look back at you? A bunch, that's the point here.

We have Jesus' words in the gospel of Mark, *"**<u>Whoever</u>** wants to be my disciple must deny themselves and take up their cross and follow me"* Mark 8:34. The "whoever" in this context means anyone. It's a comprehensive offer to the whole world.

We learn from Peter this same thing, *"The Lord is not slow in keeping his promise, as some understand slowness. Instead, he is patient with you, not wanting **anyone** to perish, but **everyone** to come to repentance."* (2 Peter 3:9)

I point this out because many think and feel that God doesn't want anything to do with them. They feel they are too far gone or that God isn't interested in their life at all. And that simply is not true. If you feel that way just look back at these promises from the Bible. These Bible passages of Scripture assure us that God's plan of redemption is for everyone, including you!

As we move into verse seven, we notice that redemption is comprehensive in its role in our daily life.

In its Role

"So <u>walk</u> in him, ⁷<u>rooted</u> and <u>built up</u> in him and <u>established</u> in the faith, just as you were taught." v 6-7

Notice how Paul develops powerful word pictures to illustrate the comprehensive nature of what redemption does to our character. As we allow Christ to move and work through us, we become "rooted," "built up," and "established." This character development program is driven by our day-to-day actions. Paul says it this way, "So walk in him." The obvious implication is a step-by-step journey. We don't leap, skip, wander, saunter, or mosey our way to Christ-like character. Nope, we simply walk one step after another. Consistently moving forward.

Let's see how it's described in other passages, *"I therefore, a prisoner for the Lord, urge you to **walk in a manner worthy** of the*

Freedom

calling to which you have been called." (Ephesians 4:1)

Early on in this letter to the Colossians, Paul says, "I haven't stopped praying for you, *"so that you may **live a life worthy** of the Lord and please him in every way: **bearing fruit** in every good work, **growing in the knowledge** of God."* (Colossians 1:10)

To another emerging congregation in Thessalonica, Paul writes, *"We pleaded with you, encouraged you, and urged you to **live your lives in a way that God would consider worthy**."* (1 Thess 2:12)

We can see in all these passages the same pattern and strategy. Becoming a strong, stable, and thriving Christian doesn't magically happen. No, it happens over time as we become rooted, built up, and established in Him.

This establishment of our faith, because of our redemption, results in a life of thanksgiving. We have a redemption that is comprehensive in its results.

In its Results

*"⁶Therefore, as you received Christ Jesus the Lord, so walk in him, ⁷rooted and built up in him and established in the faith, just as you were taught, **abounding** in thanksgiving."* Colossians 2:6-7

Paul mentions *"**abounding** in thanksgiving"* after verse seven. The structure of the verse points to the obvious conclusion that one who is redeemed, thereby walking in Christ, is blessed with the benefit of being like a tree firmly planted. Interestingly, a wild fig tree growing in Echo Caves near Ohrigstad, South Africa has roots going 120 m (400 ft) deep, giving it the deepest roots known of any tree.[69] That's the kind of spiritual depth that is provided for us as we walk in Christ.

This leads to a heart abounding in thanksgiving. Is it any surprise that the Bible instructs us to give thanks? "Give thanks in all circumstances; for this is the will of God in Christ Jesus for you," Paul writes in 1 Thessalonians 5:18. This phrase, *"Give Thanks,"* is found 128 times in 62 verses in the Bible. The follower of Christ can give thanks in any circumstance because the 20 to 30 feet of wind, rain, and cold can't affect the 400 feet of depth beneath your feet. You're firmly established! Have you ever met a mature believer who isn't filled with a happy and thankful heart? I haven't, and I bet you haven't either. This should tell us something. The way to thankfulness is through Christ-like maturity. That's why our redemption is comprehensive!

The next part of the text teaches us that not only is our redemption comprehensive, but it is also clear. Let's look at verse eight.

A Redemption that is Clear

"⁸See to it that no one takes you captive by philosophy and empty deceit, according to human tradition, according to the elemental spirits of the world, and not according to Christ." Colossians 2:8

The one thing you notice about God and His Word is a clear message of love for His creation. Included in that love is a clear message to us about finding our way home. We know that home to be our relationship with God through Christ. I remember growing up in the upper Midwest and the many winter days when snow and slush covered the windows of our car. If you've ever lived in a snowy climate, you know exactly what I'm talking about. Before you even get in to drive, you must find a broom or snow removal brush and clean the snow off. If you don't, you're not going anywhere! Well, the same thing is true in our understanding of our redemption. If we can't see clearly what redemption is and how it impacts our day-to-day life, then we really are never moving forward in the direction God has for us. Paul spends a couple of verses explaining to the Colossians how to get the ideologies of worldly principles off our spiritual windows. The Bible helps us to see clearly through at least two diabolic tendencies. These tendencies didn't fade out after the first century, and we must be on the lookout for them even today. The first snowstorm the Bible warns us of is the philosophies of human tradition.

Philosophical Traditions

Notice the sentence structure of this verse. Paul is warning these new believers not to be taken captive (intellectually & spiritually speaking) by philosophy (and/or empty deceit). But he continues by including a two-part categorization of *"according to human tradition"* or *"the elemental spirits of the world."* Concerning the philosophies of human tradition, we must be on guard not to bring into our spiritual life that which is contrary to the clear teaching of God's Word. There are many clever teachings, riddled traditions, and deceitful training in and out of the church world.

The astute believer doesn't have to know and understand each errand philosophy but should be able to spot a fraud when confronted with it. In the working out of our salvation, the Christian is wise to compare all suggested spiritual practices, ideologies, or beliefs to and against Scripture. In doing this, we are following

Paul's instructions to the Corinthians, where he writes, *"⁵We destroy arguments and every lofty opinion raised against the knowledge of God, and take every thought captive to obey Christ."* (2 Corinthians 10:5) The encouragement to us is not to add anything to our salvation beyond putting our whole faith and trust in Jesus Christ.

There is another word of encouragement provided to us in the Bible regarding this point. Look how Paul describes it to the Christians in the city of Corinth, *"⁴In their case the god of this world has blinded the minds of the unbelievers, to keep them from seeing the light of the gospel of the glory of Christ, who is the image of God."* (2 Corinthians 4:4) We see here that spiritual blindness comes over those who do not know Christ. It's like we mentioned early; there's snow on their windshield. So, the question becomes, why in the world would I listen to someone telling me how to drive my car when the windows are completely covered in snow? I'd be crazy. They have no idea which way to go. In fact, if I listened to their advice, the most likely and most certain outcome would be a crash. So don't let people who teach outside of the clear understanding of God's Word influence your redemption. The Bible is your snow removal device, and don't use anything else! The second snowstorm the Bible warns us of is mystical deceptions.

Mystical Deceptions

The second category of falseness pointed out by this passage is the deception of mystical ideas. Paul uses the phrase *"empty deceit"* in reference to *"the elemental spirits of the world."* Many wonder, what does that mean? The basic reference is simply understood. The most likely idea is it means the basic functioning of our world. We could think of the physical properties of the world in this case. For example, you may be aware of some religious systems that worship the earth, wind, water, and sky. Also attached to this idea are certain types of numerological structures that were associated with the ethereal systems during the first century. The false teachers in Colossae were instructing believers to trust in mathematical systems of behavior as they related to lifestyle and other personal disciplines. The hope was that if one were to keep the 'proper' order, then spiritual emanations from other worlds would bring favor to those keeping these rigid tactics, hence the word "spirit" in lowercase.

This isn't the only time Paul dealt with this issue. A passage in the book of Galatians provides a second point of view on this phrase. Paul writes, *"³In the same way we also, when we were children, were enslaved to the elementary principles of the world... ⁹But now that you have come to know God, or rather to be known by God, how can you turn back again to the weak and worthless elementary principles of the world, whose slaves you want to be once more?"* (Galatians 4:3,9) This passage utilizes the same style and format in the original language as we find in the letter to the Colossians. This helps us to strip away any far-fetched ultra-mystical meanings to the phrase. Most biblical scholars conclude the *"spiritual elements"* and *"elementary principles"* have the same meaning in these two letters.

What that means for us is we don't have to get caught up in the deception of otherworldly manifestations or ultra-rigid lifestyle requirements in order to deepen, secure, or protect our free gift of salvation. We have a redemption that was paid for by Christ, and there's nothing to be added to it.

Mystery of Christ

Paul wraps up this small section by emphasizing we have a clear view of Jesus as our pathway to redemption. Yet, within this understanding, we come to realize that to the outside world, we are declaring a mystery. Later in his letter, Paul requests prayer as he continues his ministry while in a Roman prison. Here is his plea, *"³At the same time, pray also for us, that God may open to us a door for the word, to declare the mystery of Christ, on account of which I am in prison"* Colossians 4:3. This points to the fact that without the revelation of God none of us would have a clear picture of redemption. This brings us to a place of great thankfulness and adoring worship. This point was brought out to the disciples by Jesus in the Gospel of Luke, *"¹⁰he said, "To you it has been given to know the secrets of the kingdom of God, but for others they are in parables, so that 'seeing they may not see, and hearing they may not understand"* Luke 8:10. If you know Christ and have a clear understanding of redemption, be thankful because this clarity is a gift and should draw us to worship, prayer, and the desire to use kindness when sharing our faith. It's a great reminder that many of the objections, anger, or confusion we experience when sharing our faith aren't necessarily about our ability to present the message. In many cases, God's been working or hasn't started working on the other end first. This is His plan as to when the Gospel will be revealed to the listener. Our job is to pray, look for opportunities, and when given, we present with our whole heart!

We've learned so far that we have a redemption that is

comprehensive and a redemption that is clear, next let's focus on how our redemption is complete.

A Redemption that is Complete

"⁹For in him the whole fullness of deity dwells bodily, ¹⁰and you have been filled in him, who is the head of all rule and authority. ¹¹In him also you were circumcised with a circumcision made without hands, by putting off the body of the flesh, by the circumcision of Christ, ¹²having been buried with him in baptism, in which you were also raised with him through faith in the powerful working of God, who raised him from the dead." Colossians 2:9-12

The first transcontinental flight across the country from New York, NY, to Long Beach, CA, was completed by American aviation pioneer Cal P. Rodgers in an early Wright flyer called the Vin Fiz, named after a soft drink company that sponsored the trip. On September 17, 1911, he left Sheephead Bay in Brooklyn, NY, and arrived in California on December 10, 1911, 84 days later. Rodgers actual time in the air was three days, 10 hours, and 14 minutes. The airplane was forced down by weather and mechanical failure more than 30 times, resulting in "light crashes" and some real crashes that required major repairs. When Rodgers landed in Long Beach, the only original parts on the airplane were the rear rudder and the oil pan on the engine. At least he completed the trip!

As a pastor, sometimes I hear people share a similar type of story, but it's not related to a transcontinental flight; rather, it's related to what they think things will be like for them in Heaven. When reading that story, it's easy to think about the similarities between the pilot's experience and the way we experience life on this planet. We crash, get blown off course, run out of gas, and are in desperate need of 'new parts' all the time. Because of this, many people think they'll be limping into heaven in a broken-down, pieced-together life held in place by duct tape and super glue. But in reality, nothing could be further from the truth. According to this next portion of the text, as Christians, we have a redemption that is complete. We're not going to be limping into the gates of heaven, no way! We're going to be soaring across the finish line when we get there! How do I know that? Because it's not based on my flight, my aircraft, or my resources. My eternal security and experience are based upon His equipment, His flight path, and His resources. We've got this backward. When I get saved, I'm not flying my plane anymore. I'm riding in the back seat, and God's the pilot, and He's bringing me home on His plane. Paul moves into a three-part explanation regarding the person, power, and promises of our redemption. By doing so, we will be encouraged to know that our redemption is complete!

In His Personage

In verses 9 and 10, we learn that the entirety of God rests in Christ. There isn't one part or portion of Jesus that was not and is not God. This phrase, *"in him the whole fullness of deity dwells bodily,"* means exactly that. Jesus wasn't partially God; He wasn't almost God. He wasn't nearly God. Jesus was wholly God in all fullness and in His earthly body. This is a complete manifestation of God in the flesh. This was not a partial revelation, an almost revelation, a close enough revelation of God to mankind. This was a full, complete, certain, nothing to be revealed later type of revelation. So, when we say our redemption is complete by His personage, that's what we mean.

By His Power

In verse 10, Jesus is revealed as *"the head of all rule and authority."* Paul is saying that Jesus is the complete power and ruler of everything. So, we learn that complete redemption is not only provided by Him but is powered by Him as well. We catch a second glimpse of this same point in verse 12 as Paul writes, *"the powerful working of God"* as he connects this to our baptism and eventual resurrection from the grave. There is no mistake in Scripture that Jesus maintains all authority and power above and over all things. So, if we think we are going to only squeak by over the finish in heaven, we are essentially telling God that He doesn't have the power to work out His plan in my life.

But there is a greater point to be made here. Something that transcends the talk of power. It's the very essence that drives His power underneath it all. Legend has it that a wealthy merchant traveling through the Mediterranean world looking for the distinguished Pharisee, Paul, encountered Timothy, who arranged a visit. Paul was, at the time, a prisoner in Rome. Stepping inside the cell, the merchant was surprised to find a rather old man, physically frail, but whose serenity and magnetism challenged the visitor. They talked for hours. Finally, the merchant left with Paul's blessing. Outside the prison, the concerned man inquired, "What is the secret of this man's power? I have never seen anything like it before."

Did you not guess?" replied Timothy. "Paul is in love."

T.K. Anderson

The merchant looked bewildered. "In Love?"

"Yes," the missionary answered, "Paul is in love with Jesus Christ."

The merchant looked even more bewildered. "Is that all?"

Smiling, Timothy replied, "Sir, that is everything."

Many people fear the power of God, but that doesn't need to be the case. God's power is driven by His love for you. You don't need to fear God's power. As you embrace His love for you, His power will continue to grow deeper and wider as the year's progress. And you'll be 'in love' with Jesus in a similar way as the story upholds. That's why we say we have a redemption that is complete. We've learned that we have a redemption that is complete because of the personage and power of Christ, and finally, we will consider the promises of our redemption. We have a redemption that is complete...

In its Promises

Verses 11 and 12 provide three promises that come to us through our redemption. Paul uses the illustrations of circumcision, baptism, and death to remind us of another clear picture of what Christ has already provided for us. Circumcision is the illustration Paul uses to remind us that because of the death of Jesus upon the cross, and the presence of the Holy Spirit in our life, when we are redeemed, we are now free from the old nature controlling us. We are no longer under the power of sin in our life. We won't be totally free from the old nature until we take up our new immortal body, but in the meantime, we have been freed from the old nature's control. We now have access to the Fruit of the Spirit and the ability, or free will, to decide on the right course of action.

Paul then uses baptism to remind us of the promise that our sins have been buried in the ground as Christ was buried in the tomb. This is an important promise because it means that when we come to Christ, our redemption puts away our sins. All of it. The past, the present, and the future. It's all dead and buried. That's why water baptism is such a cool reminder for us of the promise and reality of total forgiveness.

Lastly, Paul reminds us of Jesus' resurrection from the dead. Jesus' physical and bodily resurrection from the dead is a promise to us that we, too, will one day be risen to new life. The Bible is very clear that one day; these mortal bodies will *"take on immortality."* This great promise is found in Paul's letter to the Corinthians. In it, he writes, *"53For this perishable body must put on the imperishable, and this mortal body must put on immortality."* (1 Corinthians 15:5)

All these promises help us in our time of need. We need God's promises to sustain us when we're feeling down, depressed, or disappointed. When that happens, pull out your Bible and read these promises again. As you do, you'll sense the Lord's presence in your time of need. But I must tell you when He shows up in your life, He may surprise you, as Tolstoy kindly reminds us.

Martin, the Cobbler, is Leo Tolstoy's story about a lonely shoemaker who is promised in a dream that Christ will come to visit his shop. The next day Martin rises early, gets his shop ready, prepares a meal, and waits. The only one who showed up in the morning was an old beggar who came by and asked for rest. Martin gave him a room he had prepared for his divine guest. The only one to show up in the afternoon was an old lady with a heavy load of wood. She was hungry and asks for food. He gave her the food he had prepared for his divine guest. As evening came, a lost boy wandered by. Martin took him home, afraid all the while that he would miss Christ. That night in his prayers, he asks the Lord, "Where were You? I waited all day for You."

The Lord said to Martin:

Three times I came to your friendly door, Three times my shadow was on your floor. I was a beggar with bruised feet. I was the woman you gave to eat. I was the homeless child on the street.

What a wonderful reminder that the promises of our redemption are not only for us as we are encouraged to continue to share the message of God's love to a world that so desperately needs it. Finally, we come to the conclusion of this text and here we find redemption that cancels our debt.

A Redemption that Cancels our Debt

"[13]And you, who were dead in your trespasses and the uncircumcision of your flesh, God made alive together with him, having forgiven us all our trespasses, [14]by canceling the record of debt that stood against us with its legal demands. This he set aside, nailing it to the cross. [15]He disarmed the rulers and authorities and put them to open shame, by triumphing over them in him." Colossians 2:13-15

Freedom

After meditating on several Scriptures, an attorney decided to cancel the debts of all his clients who owed him money for more than 6 months. He drafted a letter explaining his decision and its biblical basis and sent 17 debt-canceling letters via certified mail. One by one, the letters were returned by the Postal Service, unsigned and undelivered. Perhaps a couple of people had moved away, though not likely. Sixteen of the seventeen letters came back to him because the clients refused to sign for and open the envelopes, fearing that this attorney was suing them for their debts. How profound! We owe a debt for our sins, and God is willing to cancel it, but too many people will not even open the letter that explains how.

The good news of the Gospel is that while we were far away from God and with no interest or way to come back, He pursued us. That's Paul's first point in this next section of our text. Our redemption cancels our debt even when we are far away.

Like the attorney who decided to cancel the debts unannounced to those who were indebted to him, God decided to release us of our sinful debt against us. Verse 13 points this out by explaining, *"you, who were dead in your trespasses,"* tells us that we were lifeless in our sins. Our spiritual life was dead. Our existence was hopeless. Our eternal separation from God was sealed. But then something happened. Christ came to earth and paved a new way for us. Redemption was purchased by His sacrifice. Because of this great sacrifice, we now have a life with Christ.

Paul continues by writing it this way, *"God made alive together with him, having forgiven us all our trespasses."* Don't miss the impact of this important truth. You see, in every religious system, the deity never comes after the lost, the fallen, the guilty, or the unredeemable. In fact, it's the complete opposite. The lost are banished, cut off, and destroyed. But, in Christianity, we find God reaching out, searching for, and physically (literally) coming after His creation. This is a redemption that is simply beyond amazing and outside of comprehension.

The final two points of this passage are best shared with a longer-than-normal story. It's a story that shows us how God provides new life while he puts our enemies to shame. Verses 14 and 15 clearly show how the finished work of Jesus on the cross provides for us the entirety of what is needed to justify the wrath of God toward sinful man. And what I've discovered is that even though most people understand the logic of this, they have yet to fully comprehend the scope of it and the personal impact of what it means to have your debt of sin completely canceled. Many in our day simply don't believe they need a Savior. It reminds me of the following story.

A man named Gerhard Dirks, the "father of the modern computer," was one who had to face up to life's most important question. During the years of the Second World War, he made many inventions that led to the development of the first computers. He and his family escaped from Hitler's Germany and later Russian occupation to the west. He was a brilliant man, reported to have an IQ of 208. He had over 140 patents with IBM and even attempted theoretically to reconstruct the human brain. But he became completely bewildered and shaken when confronted with the complexity and utter impossibility of such a reconstruction. He didn't know what to do or where to run. He had to face a choice: Either the human brain came about by a fantastic chance or by intelligent planning. Dirks reestablished contact with an old friend and found out this friend had become a Christian. He saw the change in this man from being selfish and impatient to be patient and at peace. But Dirks clung to his atheism because he could not understand how God could know all about us, every person in the entire world. He couldn't understand where God could possibly store all the information about every person that ever lived.

Dirks went with his friend to a discussion group where a man talked about God. Someone asked, "What do you say to someone who thinks they are not a sinner?" The leader of the meeting told the man to take four pieces of paper and number them 1 to 4, and write a list of things on each piece of paper. On page 1, he said: write down every time you can remember when you said "yes" and meant "no" or said "no" and meant "yes." Then write down every time you can remember when you told an outright lie. Write down every time you gave someone a shady answer, every time you made a promise and broke it, and every time you made a promise and never intended to keep it.

On page 2, write what it is that you hide from everybody. You don't have to show this to anyone, but to yourself. And write down something that, if anyone found out about it, something inside you would wither.

On page 3, he said to make a list of friends to whom you have done something that you would not want them to do to you. Never mind if they did something to provoke you, just put down your part.

On page 4, write the names of the people for whom you have done something good, and done it without hope of any compensation or reward of any kind. He then said, "I think that any man who does that honestly will see that he is a sinner and that he is desperately in the need of salvation. He will know that the sin and the wrong he has written down is only the tip of an iceberg."

Dirks went home and did it, and the imbalance between paper 4 and papers 1, 2, and 3 was self-evident. He had to admit he was a sinner. And suddenly, it hit him. He knew where God stored data. He got his answer without even looking for it. God stored the information about Dirks IN DIRKS. Everything he had ever thought, seen, heard, said, done - everything was there in his own mind. He was his own "file." Every human being was his own "file." Now, he lost all his excuses for not believing in the Savior. People CAN change because he saw the real changes in his friend. And there is information for a final judgment - because every person carries his own data. He realized that he did not like himself and the way he lived. Just like when a computer has errors, he needed to be "debugged." He fell onto his knees and prayed, "Lord Jesus Christ, have mercy on me and wash me in your blood."

In a few minutes, he stopped crying. He knew that something had happened. A wall had come down, the wall that had stood between him and his Creator. He hadn't known the wall was there until it came down. It was the wall that Christ had demolished. Now, for the first time in his life, he knew what it meant to have fellowship with his Heavenly Father. Then he thought, it wasn't a wall; it was more like a sphere made of stone - a sphere that formed a prison. It had kept him in, and God out. He was now free of that prison!

Conclusion

If you were to go to YouTube and type in the song title "So Will I (100 Billion X)" by Hillsong United you'll quickly notice a song that

Freedom

has garnered over 175 million views since its inception four years ago. It's a powerful song with lyrics to stir the soul. One of the song's key lyrics is anchored in this idea of redemption. If fact, here's a response by the songwriters as to why they wrote it,

> *This song is about God as an artisan; this song is about God as an artist working on his masterpiece, a work of art called love. And it began with creation, and it goes through the whole story where it was finished at the cross. And now it continues to be rebirthed and restored in and through us here and now. The whole picture is a response. If the stars were made to worship so will I. You know if creation bows before You so will I. If it all exists to praise You so will I. And the more we thought about it there were just endless metaphors and pictures and things that came back to this response. And maybe nothing better than if You laid Your life down, if you gladly chose surrender, so will I. And if You left the grave behind You so will I. To us, that's everything, the entire story of why we're here and our purpose, and what it means to follow Jesus and live for Him.*[70]

One of the hardest things for us to do is to leave the grave behind us. So many times, we try to walk in new life while walking around in our old grave clothes. That's crazy! Listen friend if Christ has forgiven you then why are you still in the grave? It's time to walk out of that grave. It's time to receive the totality of your redemption and walk in the newness of life.

A little boy visiting his grandparents was given his first slingshot. He practiced in the woods but could never hit his target. As he came back to Grandma's backyard, he spied her pet duck. On an impulse, he took aim and let fly. The stone hit, and the duck fell dead. The boy panicked. Desperately he hid the dead duck in the wood pile, only to look up and see his sister watching. Sally had seen it all, but she said nothing.

After lunch that day, Grandma said, "Sally, let's wash the dishes." But Sally said, "Johnny told me he wanted to help in the kitchen today. Didn't you Johnny?" And she whispered to him, "Remember the duck!" So, Johnny did the dishes. Later, Grandpa asked if the children wanted to go fishing. Grandma said, "I'm sorry, but I need Sally to help me make supper." Sally smiled and said, "That's all taken care of. Johnny wants to do it." Again, she whispered, "Remember the duck." Johnny stayed while Sally went fishing.

After several days of Johnny doing both his chores and Sally's, finally he couldn't stand it. He confessed to Grandma that he'd killed the duck. "I know, Johnny," she said, giving him a hug. "I was standing at the window and saw the whole thing. Because I love you, I forgave you.

But I wondered how long you would let Sally make a slave of you."[71]

For some of you reading this, you need to let the past go because Jesus already has. If He's let it go, so should you. Walk in redemption and leave the grave behind.

Chapter Nine

Trust in His Restoration

Colossians 3:1-17

Leo Tolstoy wrote a story about a successful peasant farmer who was not satisfied with his lot. He wanted more of everything. One day he received a novel offer. For 1,000 rubles he could buy all the land he could walk around in a day. The only catch in the deal was that he had to be back at his starting point by sundown.

Early the next morning he started out walking at a fast pace. By midday he was very tired, but he kept going, covering more and more ground. Well into the afternoon he realized his greed had taken him far from the starting point. He quickened his pace, and as the sun began to sink low in the sky he began to run, knowing that if he did not make it back by sundown the opportunity to become an even bigger landholder would be lost. As the sun began to sink below the horizon, he came within sight of the finish line. Gasping for breath, his heart pounding, he called upon every bit of strength left in his body and staggered across the line just before the sun disappeared. He immediately collapsed, blood streaming from his mouth. In a few minutes, he was dead.

Afterward his servants dug a grave. It was not much over six feet long and three feet wide. The title of Tolstoy's story was *How Much Land Does a Man Need?* In the end, Tolstoy suggests, all a man really owns is a six-foot by three-foot piece of earth, so we are better off putting our confidence and trust elsewhere. Jesus, like Tolstoy, is warning us that we had better not put our trust in the promises of this world; we will be sadly disappointed if we do.

People trust in all sorts of things. It seems to be the case in our world that people focus on material items and individual identities the most. At the end of the line, this kind of fabricated trust is misplaced. These temporary items or individual accolades fade like the setting sun or an autumn breeze. Once the winds of change blow through our life, the important things seem a whole lot less important. The sad part is, for most people, the realization of our misplaced trust in the temporary comes too late. Don't let that happen to you.

As Paul begins to wrap up his letter to the believers in Colossae, he shares with them the importance of trusting in what Christ is doing in their lives. As the world focuses on how to best gain personal attention, attraction, or allure, God is focusing on the process of our personal restoration. God is like the ultimate restoration guru. He can take the banged-up, broken-down, and busted-up individual and turn him into a wonderful follower of Jesus that brings honor and glory to His name.

That's the emphasis of this passage. Paul is going to teach us God's restoration process. As Christians we need to relax as God begins His work in us. Too many times we think it's all on us. There are things for us to do as followers of Jesus, but the whole process of being restored is not about what we do, but about what He's already done and how He's working in our life. So if your Christian life isn't what you want it to be or hoped it to be, can I encourage you to reset your thinking and allow this section of Paul's letter to the Colossians to reenergize your heart as you learn how to trust in His restoration of your life? Let's start first with the promise of your restoration.

The Promise of Your Restoration

"¹If then you have been raised with Christ, seek the things that are above, where Christ is, seated at the right hand of God. ²Set your minds on things that are above, not on things that are on earth. ³For you have died, and your life is hidden with Christ in God. ⁴ When Christ who is your life appears, then you also will appear with him in glory." Colossians 3:1-4

The nineteenth-century evangelist, Dwight L. Moody, once said, "God never made a promise that was too good to be true." Yet people make all sorts of promises which end up either unfulfilled or unfruitful. It reminds me of a fisherman who was out of fellowship with the Lord and was at sea with his godless companions when a storm came up and threatened to sink their ship. His friends begged him to pray; but he hesitated, saying, "It's been a long time since I've done that or even entered a church." At their insistence, however, he finally cried out, "Oh Lord, I haven't asked anything of you in 15 years, and if you help us now and bring us safely to land, I promise I won't bother you again for another 15!"

Although our promises can be fickle, thankfully, when the Lord promises something, we can be assured He will back it up. In the first part of this passage, Paul begins with the word "if." And it's important for us to know that in Paul's language this would have been viewed as our word "because." In other words, when I say, *"if you would just listen to me,"* I'm conveying the hope that you will do so. But if I say, *"because you are listening to me,"* I'm conveying the fact that you are doing so. That's what Paul is saying here, *"because you have been raised"* and so on; the following I'm about to write is true. This can best be put as these are things promised to us by Christ. So that brings up the question, what is promised to the follower of Jesus?

Paul explains we are **raised** with Christ because we have **died** with Christ and have been **hidden** with Christ, and finally, we will **appear** with Christ in glory. That's a whole lot of theological gold in these four words. It could take an entire semester just to unpack the depth of spiritual truth found here. Yet for our purposes the best way to quickly understand all this is to simply remember what's taking place in the greater context of this passage. And that is to view this passage as the promise of God's restoration of our life. What would this passage have sounded like to the original readers?

Well, imagine about 2000 years ago, a small group of Jewish people living under the tyranny of Roman rule, began to listen to the words of an itinerant preacher. They saw Him reach out in love to the hurting people, the broken people, to comfort them and heal them. They heard Him give radically new interpretations of the ancient Scripture. Then they watched in horror as He was arrested, tried on trumped-up charges, beaten, mocked, spat upon, and finally nailed to a cross to die between two thieves. They experienced the incredible pain of seeing Him dead and buried on Friday and the incredible joy of seeing Him alive on Sunday.

Freedom

They heard His promise that His Spirit would remain with them all the days of their lives and beyond. And as they remembered what He had said and done, maybe they remembered the day of His baptism by John in the Jordan River. Maybe they remembered that a voice from heaven had declared, "This is my Beloved Son, in whom I am well pleased." And maybe the pieces of the puzzle began to fit a little better for them.

You see, many of these early followers of Jesus were cast out of Jerusalem by the time of Paul's Roman imprisonment. Many of the Jewish Christians were scattered into the towns and cities of Asia Minor (*modern-day Turkey*). These were cities like Philippi, Thessalonica, Corinth, and Colossae. So, as they read this portion of Paul's letter, it's not a stretch to imagine them recalling those memories and promises from Jesus about their life.

I think what Paul is doing here is providing great encouragement to the original audience. Yet because we deal with the same doubts as they did, the same encouragement can be applied to us as well. It's easy to get discouraged in our walk with Jesus. The pressures of this world can be exhausting. Our failures can often derail us in our spiritual journey. We think God might be mad at us, or that we really ticked Him off, and because we wouldn't want to be around a person like us, we project that belief onto God. We shouldn't do that. We must allow God to be God. His character and nature are far above what we could ever imagine or hope for. That's what Paul is doing here. He's reminded the Colossians that they have been **raised** with Christ in the past. They are currently **hidden** with Christ in the present, and they will **appear** with Christ in the future. All of this is a promise from God to us.

It's the same promise Paul wrote to the early believers in Rome, *"We were buried therefore with him by baptism into death, in order that, just as Christ was raised from the dead by the glory of the Father, we too might walk in newness of life."* (Romans 6:4) Again, this is important for us to know as we talk about walking in newness of life because this isn't something that we have to create or invent. This whole process of walking in a new way is God's idea and is backed by His promise.

Now that we have the promise of restoration locked down, let's move to the second aspect of this process of restoration. It's found in the plan for your restoration.

The Plan for Your Restoration

"⁵Put to death therefore what is earthly in you: sexual immorality, impurity, passion, evil desire, and covetousness, which is idolatry. ⁶On account of these the wrath of God is coming. ⁷In these you too once walked, when you were living in them. ⁸But now you must put them all away: anger, wrath, malice, slander, and obscene talk from your mouth. ⁹Do not lie to one another, seeing that you have put off the old self with its practices." Colossians 3:5-9

President Dwight Eisenhower once said, "In preparing for battle, I have always found that plans are useless, but planning is indispensable." That's great wisdom from a perceptive leader. Isn't it true that life and situations rarely go the way we plan. But more often than not, if we haven't planned ahead we find ourselves in a heap of trouble. This can be true in our business life and personal life. What we're finding here in the second section of this passage is a reminder to plan ahead when considering how to walk in this newly restored life. Someone once said, "If you don't design your own life plan, chances are you'll fall into someone else's plan." That's exactly what our enemy, the devil, would like for us to do. He wants us to fall into his plan by not planning ahead.

You'll notice these three phrases, *"put to death," "put them all away,"* and *"put off the old self,"* are included in this plan. Paul does a great job in verses 5 through 9 dividing out for us the difference between individual actions that harm us and others-based actions that harm as well. In the middle, however, you might have noticed a hinge statement in verse 7, "In these you too once walked, when you were living in them." Did you notice that part? It's important because these actions are not something that has control over us anymore. Because we have the power of Christ and the presence of the Holy Spirit working in us, we are no longer slaves to or bound by these actions.

When we become Christians the old nature doesn't disappear (I wish it did), it lingers. It reminds me of a story I heard about a guy on trial for murder, but the prosecution couldn't find a body. According to the story, there was strong evidence of guilt, but there was no corpse. In the defense's closing statement, the lawyer, knowing his client would probably be convicted, resorted to a trick.

"Ladies and gentlemen of the jury, I have a surprise for you all," the lawyer said as he looked at his watch. "Within one minute, the person presumed dead in this case will walk into this courtroom." He looked toward the courtroom door. The jurors, somewhat stunned, all looked on eagerly.

A minute passed. Nothing happened.

Finally, the lawyer said, "Actually, I made up the previous statement. But you all looked on with anticipation. I, therefore, put it to you that you have a reasonable doubt in this case as to whether anyone was killed, and I insist that you return a verdict of not guilty."

The jury retired to deliberate. A few minutes later, the jury returned and pronounced a verdict of guilty.

"But how?" inquired the lawyer. "You must have had some doubt; I saw all of you stare at the door."

The jury foreman replied: "Yes, we did look, but your client didn't."

How true it is. We all know our old nature is still alive and kicking inside of us. We would like to think we've conquered all our habits and hang-ups, but if we're brutally honest, we still struggle. The Bible doesn't say we're cured of our sinful tendencies when we get saved; it simply teaches that we are not under the bondage of our old nature. That's a big difference. It means we can be free, but only if we begin making the right choices to "put away" those activities and actions contrary to God's nature.

So what are we to put off? We are to put off, or put away, our acts relating to us as an individual and our actions that relate to our interaction with others. First, we're to put away "immorality, impurity, passion, evil desire, and covetousness." Next, we're to put away "anger, wrath, malice, slander, obscene talk, and lying." As I mentioned earlier, we can see that one set of items relates to our internal condition and the other set of items relates to our external condition. In both cases we have a clear direction from the

Bible to put away these actions. It's interesting to note that the Bible does not teach that God will put away these actions for us. Why doesn't He do that for us? The answer is simple. If He put away these actions, then we would be stripped of our free will. It would be the same thing if God automatically forced every person to believe in Him and follow Him in worship and adoration. If God did that we'd be nothing more than flesh and bone robots. God doesn't want that. Part of the human experience is learning how to experience God and get to know Him, at least in part now, but in whole throughout eternity.

The plan regarding our restoration couldn't be clearer. We have a part in this story. Putting away the practices of our old life will not be easy, but it is attainable. The good news is that beyond this plan we come to the next element embedded within our process of restoration, the product of restoration.

The Product of Your Restoration

*"[10]and have **put on the new self**, which is being renewed in knowledge after the image of its creator. [11]Here there is not Greek and Jew, circumcised and uncircumcised, barbarian, Scythian, slave, free; but Christ is all, and in all. [12]Put on then, as God's chosen ones, holy and beloved, compassionate hearts, kindness, humility, meekness, and patience, [13]bearing with one another and, if one has a complaint against another, forgiving each other; as the Lord has forgiven you, so you also must forgive. [14]And above all these put on love, which binds everything together in perfect harmony. [15]And let the peace of Christ rule in your hearts, to which indeed you were called in one body. And be thankful. [16]Let the word of Christ dwell in you richly, teaching and admonishing one*

another in all wisdom, singing psalms and hymns and spiritual songs, with thankfulness in your hearts to God." Col 3:10-16

A pastor stood up at a Rotary Club when it was his turn to speak and said:

> I'm with a global enterprise. We have branches in every country in the world. We have our representatives in nearly every parliament and boardroom on earth. We're into motivation and behavior alteration. We run hospitals, feeding stations, crisis pregnancy centers, universities, publishing houses, and nursing homes. We care for our clients from birth to death.
>
> We are into life insurance and fire insurance. We perform spiritual heart transplants. Our original Organizer owns all the real estate on earth, plus an assortment of galaxies and constellations. He knows everything and lives everywhere. Our product is free for the asking. (There's not enough money to buy it.) Our CEO was born in a hick town, worked as a carpenter, didn't own a home, was misunderstood by his family, hated by enemies, walked on water, was condemned to death without a trial, and arose from the dead. I talk with him every day.

The impact of Jesus can be seen in the lives of those who follow Him. Their impact is the product of God's restoration process. But it's important to remember, this isn't an automatic thing. According to verse 10, we are to "put on" our new self through a different set of actions and activities within our life.

Now that we've put off the old self, Paul reminds us to put on the new self. Again, this is a specific action or activity to be done by us. God isn't going to cause us to choose the right action in a way that is against our free will. But He will provide us with renewed knowledge of what to do. Did you catch that in verse 10, "Put on the new self, which is being renewed in knowledge after the image of its creator." This is where the process of restoration picks up positive steam.

I just love hearing the stories of men and women who come to Christ, and their lives are changed instantly. You hear their stories of how they used to be involved in all sorts of harmful lifestyle choices, addictions, or behaviors. But once Christ becomes Lord and Savior, it's like a switch goes on, and those old, former desires simply fade away because a new and greater desire to please God overtakes them. They acquire new "knowledge" of what to do.

I remember when I decided to commit my life to Jesus at the age of 16. It was a very interesting time in my life, but I knew God was working on me and I knew that I wanted to be a part of His kingdom in this world. Yet like a normal teenager, I had developed some unhealthy habits. I don't need to go into all the details, but suffice it to say that anger and foul language were not uncommon for me and my sphere of former friends.

The most interesting thing happened once I rededicated my life to Jesus in a simple prayer; God heard me, He met me, and He changed me instantly. In fact, within a couple of days many of my former friends kept asking me, "What happened to you? You're different. You've changed." The difference was obvious and instant. I no longer used foul language, and almost instantly, the intense anger that once drove my life was gone. There's not a person on the planet that could convince me otherwise because it happened to me. It happened in me. It happened through me.

It reminds me of a story in the gospel of John about a blind man who was healed by Jesus. The religious leaders were trying to figure out what happened. They wanted to analyze the man's experience, but I just love the blind man's response. He said, "(Jesus) put mud on my eyes, and I washed, and (now) I see." But the Pharisees said, "This man (Jesus) is not from God, for he does not keep the Sabbath." But others said, "How can a man who is a sinner do such signs?" And there was a division among them." Yet still, the religious leaders could not come to a conclusion, "So for the second time they called the man who had been blind and said to him, "We know that this man (Jesus) is a sinner." He answered, "Whether he is a sinner I do not know. One thing I do know, that though I was blind, now I see." (John 9:13-25)

You see, skeptics always have a difficult time believing the story of one who has been touched by God. But for the ones whom God has changed, they never have a difficult time sharing their story. Have you shared your story lately? If not, begin looking for opportunities to share your story because there are many people in your sphere of influence who need to hear how God has changed you into the person you are today.

As you read through verses 10 through 16, you pick up many things that we are to put on with our new knowledge. The main emphasis in verse 11 is that the dividing walls of nationality, culture, and social status have all been removed for those within the Body of Christ. Because of His finished work upon the cross we should now be the product of His love. As His product of love we now display actions of humility, kindness, forgiveness, forbearance, compassion, and the list continues. I counted eight specific actions all wrapped up in the attitude of love.

Finally, in verse 16, we find the ultimate result of our product in a community of like-minded people who uphold each other in spiritual maturity. Paul concludes, "Let the word of Christ dwell in you richly, teaching and admonishing one another in all wisdom, singing psalms and hymns and spiritual songs, with thankfulness in your hearts to God." What an amazing picture of the Body of Christ functioning in unity. This type of relational quality warms the heart of God and brings joy to us as a result.

We come to the final part of God's great restoration project, and it concludes with the purpose of your restoration. Why does God do all of this? What's the purpose?

The Purpose of Your Restoration

"*17And whatever you do, in word or deed, do everything in the name of the Lord Jesus, giving thanks to God the Father through him."* Colossians 3:17

"Lucy, I need help," Charlie Brown says woefully. "What can I do for a purpose in life?"

Lucy responds, "Oh, don't worry, Charlie. It's like being on a big ocean liner making its way through the sea. Some folks put their deck chairs to face the bow of the ship, and others place their chairs to face the side of the ship or the back of the ship. Which way do you face, Charlie?"

Charlie Brown concludes sadly, "I can't even unfold the deck chair."

Life feels like that sometimes, doesn't it? We look around us and everyone seems to be doing well and going someplace in life. We evaluate our life against theirs and seem to be stuck in the same spot. Well, God doesn't have that in mind for you and me. He wants us to have a life of abundance, a life of purpose, a life of dynamic impact for His kingdom. I love what Jesus said, *"The thief comes only to steal and kill and destroy. I came that they may have life and have it abundantly."* (John 10:10) Satan wants to destroy you. Jesus wants to grow you.

Some people go through their entire life never knowing that God has a design and purpose for their life all along. By not getting in tune with God's frequency, they miss out on the wonderful elements prepared in advance for them. Paul concludes this passage we've been studying by emphasizing the overarching reason for God's plan of restoration. God restores us so that we can bring glory back to Him. Did you catch that in verse 17? We are to give "thanks to God the Father through (Jesus)." And this includes everything we do. Not some things, many things, a few things, but all things. Look how Paul wrote it, "Whatever you do, in word or deed, do everything in the name of the Lord Jesus." That's a pretty comprehensive list, isn't it? I wonder how much of everything it includes. Sounds like everything, doesn't it?

When teaching this type of passage after having been a teacher of God's Word for over two decades, I often get questions about what this really means to the average person. Does Paul really mean everything that we do? Are there any exceptions? Obviously he's not referring to tying shoes or taking out the trash or other menial tasks of each day. After all, Paul told the Christians in Corinth a similar thing, *"So, whether you eat or drink, or whatever you do, do all to the glory of God."* (1 Corinthians 10:31) But how do we draw a distinction, and are "all things" (things that we do) to be caught up in this phrase? I heard a story a long time ago that humorously illustrates this discussion point,

In the late 1800s in the eastern part of Tennessee, there was a famous moonshiner known as Big Haley. The woman's real name was Mahala Mullins, but since she weighed somewhere around 500 pounds, "Big Haley" was not an inappropriate name.

Big Haley and her sons ran a reliable operation. They were renowned for the quality of their product. They didn't dilute their moonshine and were known to deal honestly. That fact, coupled with the problems of arresting a mountain clan, caused local government officials to leave them alone.

However, a newly elected sheriff did once attempt to arrest Mahala and make a name for himself. The judge who signed the arrest warrant just smiled and told the sheriff to be sure to bring her in. The sheriff and his deputies had no trouble finding Mahala's cabin. He knocked on the cabin door, entered, and informed Mahala she was under arrest.

What he discovered, though, was that Mahala was bigger than the cabin's doorway. After some futile efforts, he decided not to arrest her after all. When the judge later asked the sheriff about Mahala, the officer complained that, "She's catchable but not fetchable." Some things in life are like that. They may be catchable, but in the vernacular of the mountains, they are not fetchable.[72]

T.K. Anderson

As I said, this is a humorous story to consider regarding this discussion. The point is that there are many things we do every day that aren't fetchable, so to speak. So in "those things," we just live in a normal way. However, the catchable things we do, like the actions and attitudes talked about in verses 10 through 16, those are the things we are to work on. When we put off the old man, we give thanks. When we put on the new self, we give thanks. When God is using our lives to impact others, we give thanks. That's what Paul is talking about here. He's not talking about when we trim our nails or snore during our sleep. He's talking about how we live out the character and nature of Christ by putting away the old man and living in the ways of our new man.

When we do that we bring glory to God. Let's take another look at that verse to those in the city of Corinth, *"So, whether you eat or drink, or whatever you do, do all to the glory of God."* (1 Cor 10:31) Clearly. the emphasis is on "Do all to the glory of God" and not necessarily on specific actions and attitudes. And we learn from other passages that our chief aim in life is to bring glory to God. But how do we do that? I like this summary, "To glorify God means to make visible or to demonstrate the majesty of God's presence, His perfections, and His work in creation, redemption, and in new creation. Man glorifies God actively by living a life in gratitude to God for His redemptive work, both in its accomplishment and application."[73] Hopefully that provides you with a foundation on what it means to glorify God.

The greater point here is that God's restoration of our life is accomplished so that we can experience abundant life, but more importantly through our abundant life God would be glorified. That's the purpose, that's the goal, that's the finish line!

Conclusion

As we conclude this chapter we consider what it means to be a part of God's ultimate restoration work. We learned there are four valuable elements regarding this grand project of individual restoration. We learned that God is interested in us on an individual and corporate level. He doesn't look at the entire world as one big blob of humanity. No, He looks at each individual in a unique and special way. We learned that God provides a promise, a plan, a product, and a purpose to restoration and that we are the ones who partner in this process as we bring glory to Him. We learned that God doesn't force our will but does provide the power, access, and willpower to change us into the person He designed us to be. Finally we discovered that abundant life comes from Jesus, as we keep our actions, attitudes, and attention focused on Him.

I have to say, however, if you don't know Jesus as your personal Lord and Savior then none of this will make sense to you. It all starts with humbling yourself before God and inviting Jesus into your life to save you and remake you. Only Jesus can save you from your sins. Only Jesus can restore you into the person you were designed to be from the start. God loves you and He wants to restore you. Will you invite Him into your life today?

In 1988, sixteen-year-old Anissa Ayala was diagnosed with a rare form of Leukemia. The doctors said that if she did not receive a bone marrow transplant after chemotherapy and radiation treatment, she would die.

Neither her parents nor her brother were a match, and they could not find a donor elsewhere. Her parents, both in their forties, conceived another child and hoped that her bone marrow would be compatible with Anissa's.

To their great delight, it was determined that this new baby was a compatible donor, and when Marissa Ayala was fourteen months old, they took some of her marrow and gave it to Anissa. Anissa made a full recovery from Leukemia, and both sisters lead healthy lives today.

In a sense, Marissa saved her sister's life. She says, "Without me being a perfect match for my sister, she would not be here."[74]

Jesus was born into this world for the express purpose of saving us. He is the one and only Savior that can save all those who put their trust in Him. Every God-honoring action points people to Him. When we live out our newly restored life through Him, we are telling the entire world that without Jesus, we would not have salvation. And that brings glory to God.

The Interlude between Colossians and Philemon

As the weeks and months of Paul's two-year ordeal wore on, we can almost be certain that he was both enlarging his influence and longing to have a hearing before the Emperor of Rome. The productivity of his writing, along with the salvation of many of those in Caesar's household, kept him energized during this time, but the confinement of his location may have started to show. A guy like Paul loved to be out and about, traveling the Mediterranean region, and sharing the gospel without hindrance. So as he waits, he entertains his visitors and looks for ways in which he can still impact the early church through his ministry of writing.

One of his recent visitors was a man named Onesimus, a visitor with a rather sorted past. Onesimus was a runaway slave of his friend Philemon. Paul doesn't shy away from the issue of slavery and how to handle it in a biblical way. This is true for all generations of Christ followers. We face cultural issues in our time as well, and we should not back away from addressing those issues in a way that is Christ-focused and honoring to our Savior. The solution for Paul isn't to issue a political statement, call a press conference, or protest for change to upend the entire Roman Empire. After all, it was an empire of some 60,000,000 slaves during the time of Paul.

Paul's approach is the same as Jesus' approach; he looks at the issue from the perspective of an individual and asks, "What should be done in this specific situation?" Change is always best done when it occurs in the heart of an individual and not through a decree or an impersonal edict. People tend to fight against decrees because a heart can't be legislated. But when we decide to follow the way of Jesus, that's when real change takes place. It was true in this letter to Philemon, and it's still true today.

We can't be certain about the order in which each of these four prison letters was written, but we do know that the letter to the Colossians and this personal letter to Philemon must have been written within the same timeframe because they were delivered as a set to the church in Colossae. Yet, although delivered together, this letter was a personal correspondence between Paul and Philemon. In fact, it's the only personal letter that we have of Paul to an individual. No doubt he wrote others, but the Holy Spirit saw fit for this letter to be preserved and included in the canon of Scripture. What was the main purpose behind this letter?

There are times in life when we need to ask for a favor, especially from a friend. That's the context of the writing of this letter. Paul is friends with Philemon, yet Paul desires for his new covert, Onesimus, to stay with him in Rome. It appears that Paul led Onesimus to the Lord and was very helpful to Paul in his confinement. But that's not all, you see, Onesimus was Philemon's runaway slave. So Paul had a dilemma. He writes to Philemon not only asking to keep Onesimus, but also to completely forgive him as well. Paul wanted Onesimus to stay with him because Onesimus was helpful to Paul in the work of the ministry. But Paul didn't want to do things to upset or dishonor Philemon. So, he instructs Onesimus to head back to Colossae and deliver this letter of appeal to Onesimus' owner.

Freedom

Some have wondered how close Paul and Philemon were. According to verse 22, they were close enough for Paul to ask him to get a room ready for his upcoming trip, *"Prepare a guest room for me, because I hope to be restored to you in answer to your prayer."* In verse 19, Paul mentions, *"You owe me your very self."* Most likely a reference to Paul having led Philemon to saving faith while he was in that region. There was a strong history between these two men, and it's possible that Philemon was the host of the local church in Colossae.

The main reason the small letter is so important is that it shows us how Paul applied his theology to his personal life. In many of Paul's writings, we find hypothetical situations and ideas, but here we find a true-to-life story with implications, nuance, and complexity. The letter moves Paul's thinking and action beyond the hypothetical and into reality. He shows us how to put theology into practice. The three main themes of the letter are accountability for our actions, the value of showing compassion to those in the Body of Christ, and finally the importance of reconciliation with the family of God. All of this is wrapped around the greater theme of forgiveness.

T.K. Anderson

Chapter Ten

Why Forgiveness is so Powerful

Philemon 4-10

I would like to introduce to you a study of the third shortest book in the Bible that carries with it the biggest message known to mankind, the message of forgiveness. Like it or not, you'll discover that God commands us to forgive. But what if I don't want to forgive or can't find the strength to do so? I have good news that'll help you on this journey. But first, how did we get this letter?

While in a Roman jail, Paul the apostle wrote a personal letter to a friend named Philemon. He wrote him a letter as a plea for forgiveness for a new friend named Onesimus. The problem was this new friend, Onesimus, was a former slave of his old friend, Philemon. The letter is only 25 verses or 335 words in the original Greek.

So, what happened in the story? After fleeing his master, Philemon, in Colossae, Onesimus fled to Rome, where he became a Christian because of Paul. So, Paul sent him back to Philemon with this letter that bears his name. In it he asks Philemon to receive Onesimus as a *"faithful and beloved brother."* Paul offers to pay Philemon anything Onesimus had taken and bear the wrong he had done him. Onesimus was accompanied on his return by Tychicus, who was also the courier of the letter to the Colossians. (Philemon 1:16, 18)

The story of a fugitive (a Colossian slave) is a beautiful illustration of Paul's character and the transforming power of the gospel. If forgiveness is such an amazing thing, why do we fight so hard with God's command to forgive? Are we really that stubborn? Maybe we just don't like to be TOLD what to do!

As Americans, we have a myriad of opinions regarding things we like. We scarcely agree on anything anymore. Whether it's 31 flavors of ice cream, 300 channels on TV, or 3,000 unique destinations for a vacation, a multiplicity of opinions rule the day. We don't agree on politics, sports teams, style of music, entertainment, vaccines, viruses, or even theology. But, if there is one thing we have almost universal and complete agreement on, it's this; we strongly dislike anyone telling us what to do! We don't like commands. Isn't that the truth?

In fact, as Americans, one of the foundational reasons for our colonial forefather's break with the British Empire was based on their aversion to taxation without representation. "Don't Tread on Me" were the words printed onto the newly created Gadsden Flag in 1775 to represent the attitudes of the newly- formed Continental Marines.[75] We learn from history that it was one too many kingly commands that became the final straw to break the camel's back. What was that straw? The Boston Tea Party.

The incident took place because Britain's East India Company was sitting on large stocks of tea they were unable to sell in England. Consequently, it nearly went bankrupt. The King of

Freedom

England intervened and passed the Tea Act of 1773. It gave the company the right to export its merchandise directly to the colonies without paying any of the regular taxes that were imposed on the colonial merchants. With this done, the company could now undersell American merchants and monopolize the colonial tea trade. This infuriated the influential colonial merchants who feared that they would be replaced and bankrupted by a powerful monopoly.

The tea was due to land on Thursday, December 16, 1773. It was on this fateful night that the Sons of Liberty, disguised as Mohawk Indians, left a huge protest and headed towards Griffin's Wharf. This was where the three ships—The Dartmouth, the newly arrived Eleanor, and Beaver— were docked.

Barrels of tea were brought up from the hold onto the deck. The barrels were opened and the tea was dumped overboard. By morning, 90,000 lbs. of tea had been transferred from the ships to the waters of the Boston harbor.

The ports of Boston were closed by the British government who also put in place other laws, known as the Intolerable Acts, as retribution. Most historians agree it was in large part the Boston Tea Party that eventually led to the American Revolution.[76]

So let me ask you, how do you react to a command you don't like? Do you throw a mini–Boston Tea Party in your mind if it's something you disagree with? We tend to wrestle against these types of governmental decrees whether it's a command, order, rule, or law. But what do you do when it's a decree or command from God found in His Word? Do you throw it overboard like a barrel of tea into the harbor of ignorance, or embrace it as an act of humble obedience?

That's the challenge we find in this little letter from Paul to Philemon. Most of us know we are free to forgive because of what Christ has accomplished for us, but are we commanded to forgive as well? And if so, how does that shape our response to those who have wronged us or deeply hurt us?

In today's message we will look at three aspects concerning the command to forgive. The first aspect we see is that forgiveness is deeply personal. Let's look at verses 4-7.

Forgiveness is Deeply Personal

⁴"I thank my God always when I remember you in my prayers, ⁵because I hear of your love and of the faith that you have toward the Lord Jesus and for all the saints, ⁶and I pray that the sharing of your faith may become effective for the full knowledge of every good thing that is in us for the sake of Christ. ⁷For I have derived much joy and comfort from your love, my brother, because the hearts of the saints have been refreshed through you." Phil 4-7

Did you notice what Paul did in his opening thoughts? He personalized the connection between himself, Philemon, fellow Christians, and the Lord. He wants Philemon, his *"brother"* in Christ, to know he is thankful for him and grateful for his leadership within the local body of Colossae. His acknowledgment of Philemon's love, faith, and fellowship are cherished qualities within the community of faith. Paul is setting the stage for an unmistakable example of love, which is forgiveness. In this case, it will be an appeal for the forgiveness of Onesimus, the runaway slave of Philemon.

Freedom

Paul is a ministry veteran. He's traveled extensively and been trained by the sharpest philosophical and theological minds of his day. He has evangelized the masses in secularized cities and stirred the synagogue hearts of the most zealous of Hebrews. He has seen the kinds of things that eat away at a person of faith. He has experienced the reality of once-passionate followers of Christ turning and walking away. He has felt the sting of false teachers, and been burned by hateful motives and those who create a multitude of troubles behind him.

Yet through his many battles, travels, and teachings, there's one thing Paul knows for sure and that is the necessity of guarding the heart: *"See to it that no one fails to obtain the grace of God; that no 'root of bitterness' springs up and causes trouble, and by it many become defiled."* (Hebrews 12:15) That's the point here, forgiveness and bitterness are both *'roots'* that spring up within the heart of a person. In the case of forgiveness, it's the grace of God that is *'obtained.'* In the case of bitterness or unforgiveness, it's trouble that *'springs up'* and *'many become defiled'* because of it.

The Bible is clear in Galatians 5:22-23 that we are to pursue this idea of growing something called "the fruit of the Spirit" in our lives. Things like love, joy, peace, patience, kindness, goodness, faithfulness, gentleness, and self-control. It's the fruit that is beneficial to us and those around us. It's personal in both individual fulfillment and relational impact.

So, when Paul writes five positive comments in verses 4-7, it's as if he is telling Philemon, *"Hey brother, I'm proud of you! Let's keep bearing this kind of fruit because it's this kind of fruit that transforms lives."*

Let's take a look at how Paul felt about his friend, Philemon, with his five comments within four verses.

- *"I thank my God always when I remember you"*
- *"I hear of your love...that you have toward the Lord...and for all the saints"*
- *"I pray that the sharing of your faith may become effective"*
- *"I have derived much joy and comfort from your love, my brother"*
- *"The hearts of the saints have been refreshed through you"*

What Paul is doing here is setting up a hidden pledge toward these positive qualities that are on display within Philemon's life. When it comes time for the issue of forgiveness to be discussed, Paul wants his friend to remember who he is and the personal cost that bitterness or unforgiveness will exact from his life. That's the thing about forgiveness, it's deeply personal. It keeps us in a healthy place spiritually, emotionally, and in many cases physically. On the contrary, unforgiveness and resentment take a tremendous toll.

According to Dr. Steven Standiford, Chief of Surgery at the Cancer Treatment Centers of America, refusing to forgive makes people sick and keeps them that way.

He writes, "It's important to treat emotional wounds or disorders because they really can hinder someone's reactions to the treatments, even someone's willingness to pursue treatment." With that in mind, forgiveness therapy is now being used to help treat multiples diseases, including cancer.[77]

Freedom

When we choose not to forgive, it only hurts us in the long run. A little boy was sitting on a park bench in obvious pain. A man walking by asked him what was wrong. The young boy said, "I'm sitting on a bumble bee." The man urgently asked, "Then why don't you get up?" The boy replied, "Because I figure I'm hurting him more than he is hurting me!" As funny as that sounds, it's what we do sometimes. We think we're hurting the one who's stung us, yet by refusing to stand up, we're only hurting ourselves.

Now I know that some of the things we've gone through, or are currently going through, are much more serious than a sting from a bumble bee. It feels more like getting trampled by a herd of buffalo sometimes. I get it. If you're human, you've been hurt, will be hurt, and/or are currently hurting. It's part of living in a fallen world with fallen folks all around us. The tough thing about all this hurt is that hurt people continue to hurt other people. It's like the gift that keeps on giving, except it's no gift at all. So, what are we to do with all this? How do we handle all the hurt around us?

The first thing to remember is that it's personal. Meaning this idea of giving forgiveness isn't something you discuss in philosophy class. It's not an imaginary number or equation discussed in a math lecture. This thing is real, and it carries real emotions with real short-term and long-term effects. Because it's real, we can take it to God in prayer. We can search the Scriptures for answers. We can discuss our scenario with friends, family, or a counselor. The key point here is that we don't have to face it alone. It may be personal, but you don't have to be isolated.

Think of it this way: Philemon and Onesimus' issue was thought to be a private letter from Paul to Philemon, yet, by the design of

God, it was turned into the most publicly viewed letter regarding the forgiveness of a slave in the history of mankind. Your issue may be personal to you, but God and your family and friends in the Body of Christ want you to know our prayer for you is that because of forgiveness we want what was written of Philemon in vs. 7 to be said of you, *"The hearts of the saints have been refreshed through you."*

The first lesson we learn about the command of forgiveness is that it's personal. Next, we will learn that forgiveness is a Divine Principle. Let's look at verse eight.

Forgiveness is a Divine Principle

"Accordingly, though I am bold enough in Christ to command you to do what is required, ⁹Yet for love's sake I prefer to appeal to you..." Philemon 8-9

Can you hear the tension in Paul's voice? As an apostle of Christ, he has the authority to command Philemon *"to do what is required"* and forgive Onesimus of his wrongdoing and reinstate him to wholeness within the church family. But he doesn't do that. Instead, Paul appeals to Philemon to do the right thing for the sake of love for his brother and for Christ. Forgiveness is a principle from God, not a power move to control others.

In this short verse, we see and understand a requirement to forgive those who have wronged us. Now lest we think this is a stand-alone verse from Paul, let's take a look at other portions of the Bible where we find a clarification of this very principle. We will do so by asking and answering five questions to build out this divine principle of being commanded to forgive.

Freedom

QUESTION #1. Who and what should we forgive?

When Jesus gave instructions about praying, he said in Mark 11:25, *"And whenever you stand praying, forgive, if you have anything against anyone, so that your Father also who is in heaven may forgive you your trespasses."*

Did you catch that from Jesus? Anything against anyone. That's comprehensive, isn't it? There's no wiggle room in that statement. What's included in this word "anything?" I looked it up, and it means exactly what it says, anything! The same is true with the word "anyone." Who's included? Anyone, that's who! Anything and anyone. Seriously, God? Yep, seriously.

QUESTION #2. How often should we forgive?

When Jesus was teaching his disciples about forgiveness, the topic of how often we should forgive someone came up. In Matthew 18:21-22 we read, *"Then Peter came up and said to him, 'Lord, how often will my brother sin against me, and I forgive him? As many as seven times?' ²²Jesus said to him, 'I do not say to you seven times, but seventy-seven times.'"*

Peter thought he was being generous by offering to forgive his brother up to seven times. Jesus took his answer and multiplied by seventy times! Forgiveness isn't an addition type of thing, where we count out each infraction committed against us. Jesus was teaching his disciples that it's a multiplication type of thing where we practice the art of forgiveness in an exponential way.

QUESTION #3. Why should we forgive?

Here's the thing about Jesus teaching us about forgiveness and the reasons behind it. When Jesus was on the cross, literally hanging between Heaven and earth, he could see the reactions of those crucifying him. So, he knows a thing or two about being wounded, rejected, betrayed, beaten, despised, mocked, or hated and yet knowing how to handle it. The Bible captures his response in Luke 23:34, *"And Jesus said, 'Father, forgive them, for they know not what they do.' And they cast lots to divide his garments."*

The idea here is simple, yet profoundly difficult to live out. In the midst of the mockery, as they gambled for his clothing, under incredible pressure and excruciating pain, Jesus gives us this powerful example of forgiveness and the reason behind it. It's based in part on this idea that at the core level, when acting in a way that hurts another person, most of us really don't know what we are doing. In other words, because of our own wounds, misunderstandings, disjointed thinking, or other maladies of the mind, we are broken inside, truly broken. And through our brokenness we lash out and hurt those around us. Many times, we lash out at those we fear or dislike, and sadly, sometimes it's the ones we love the most.

If we were to strip away all the bravado, all the bluster, all the facades, all the failures of our image, at the base level in our deepest core, we all know we're broken and in desperate need of a Savior. And what Jesus modeled here for us is that when people hurt us, he knows and understands them at their core. As his followers, we are challenged to imitate that same understanding. As mentioned above, this is simple to understand, yet profoundly difficult to live out. And that's why we need his grace.

We now know who, what, how often, and why to forgive, so what's next?

Freedom

QUESTION #4. What's the result when we forgive?

In Luke chapter six, we find Jesus talking with his disciples as he gives a series of beatitudes. These were instructions and powerful statements about life. He covers topics like judging, condemning, giving, loving others, bearing fruit, and avoiding hypocrisy. In the midst of all this, we find a little, yet huge statement on this topic of forgiveness. We read in Luke 6:37, *"Forgive, and you will be forgiven."*

What's Jesus getting at here? A man went into the shop of a gold merchant to buy a bar of gold, and the merchant pulled out a bar of gold and said, "You go ahead and measure the bar and tell me how many inches it is. That way, we can agree on the price." The man pulled a ruler out of his pocket and said, "The bar of gold is five inches in length." "Very well," said the merchant. "That'll be $500,000 for the bar of gold." Yet the man knew he shorted the merchant by using a false ruler. It was a ruler designed to make an object shorter than it appears. But the man was happy because he added the bar of gold to his collection and made $200,000 on the merchant.

A few months later, the man ran into difficult times, and his business failed. He was forced to sell all his assets to save his family. In an act of desperation, he took all of his gold bars to the merchant in order to pay his business debts. As he laid out the ten bars of gold, each measuring seven full inches in length, he knew he had enough to pay off all of his debts. But the merchant said, "Let's go ahead and use your ruler again to measure your bars of gold, and I'll pay you what your measurement says." The man was devastated because even though he knew each bar was seven inches, his ruler would show it only to be five.

When we short-change forgiveness to others, forgiveness will be short-changed to us. That's what Jesus is saying here. In verse 38 of Luke 6, Jesus goes on to say, *"For with the measure you use it will be measured back to you."* Be generous in your forgiveness. You don't have to inflate forgiveness, puff it up, or explain away wrongdoings against you. But don't limit, restrict, or hold back anything but full forgiveness when you've been wronged. When we live out our Christian experience in this fashion, we're beginning to understand why Paul chose to appeal for forgiveness rather than command it.

QUESTION #5. What happens if we don't?

A common question I get as a pastor is, "What happens if I don't forgive?" Well, it turns out that it's not only a common question today, but it was a common question during the time of Jesus as well. Thankfully, Jesus spent some time talking to his disciples about this topic and we have a snapshot of one of his parables in Matthew 18. In the story, a king forgave one of his servants of a great debt. Yet the servant went out from the king's presence and found a fellow servant who owed him a fraction of what he owed the king. He demanded payment of the debt and refused to forgive the debt when his fellow servant asked for mercy.

The king discovered what happened and this is how Jesus describes the rest of the parable, *"Then his master summoned him and said to him, 'You wicked servant! I forgave you all that debt because you pleaded with me. [33]And should not you have had mercy on your fellow servant, as I had mercy on you?' [34]And in anger his master delivered him to the jailers, until he should pay all his debt. ³⁵So also my heavenly Father will do to every one of you, if you do not forgive your brother from your heart."* (Matthew 18:32-35)

The word picture here is captivating and stunning. The parable speaks for itself. One author said, "We can take from it that if we harbor unforgiveness in our heart, which is contrary to the heart and nature of God, then we have no place within the open range of God's kingdom. If we don't forgive, we will find ourselves locked up by our own bitterness in the dungeon of resentment." Simply put, resentment and God's presence do not go hand in hand.

This is why Paul is so steadfast for Philemon to freely and graciously forgive Onesimus. Paul wants Philemon to stay qualified to lead the church in Colossae, and he wants him to stay joyful in his relationship with all the believers. Paul is pulling for mercy because mercy gives us clarity of purpose and keeps us close to the heart of God.

So far, we have discovered that forgiveness is deeply personal and it's a divine principle. The third and most powerful aspect of understanding the command to forgive is that forgiveness has a delightful pedigree.

Forgiveness has a Delightful Pedigree

⁹"...I, Paul, an old man and now a prisoner also for Christ Jesus—¹⁰I appeal to you for my child, Onesimus, whose father I became in my imprisonment." Philemon 9-10

On May 6, 2000, with over 150,000 people in attendance, horse lovers around the world witnessed the most expensive horse in the world win the 126th running of the Kentucky Derby. According to the Los Angeles Times, for the sum of $70 million dollars, the horse named Fusaichi Pegasus was purchased by an Irish billionaire within weeks of winning this distinguished race.[78] This amount eclipsed a previous record by 30 million dollars some twenty years earlier. Within weeks of winning the Derby, not only was the world moving forward as it entered a new millennium, but the world of horse racing was propelled forward due to this record-setting purchase that still stands today. But the question remains, why would someone spend 70 million dollars to purchase a horse who had won the Kentucky Derby? The answer can be found in the word "pedigree."

Pedigree is connected to the idea of lineage, inheritance, genealogy, or heritage. From a biological standpoint, experts tell us we inherit specific traits from our parents. Things like eye color, hair color, height or blood type are referred to as inherited traits. Yet things like language, length of hair, and humor are referred to as acquired traits; traits we pick up based on our interactions with the world. The $70 million was spent in the hope that the inherited trait of speed would be passed on to the offspring of Pegasus. Unfortunately, the owner of Pegasus never came close to receiving back his record-breaking investment.

Not so with Paul. History tells us there was quite a spiritual payoff for his record-breaking investment in Onesimus. But first, let's set the stage for this connection.

According to verse ten, we see Paul must have led Onesimus to the Lord while in captivity. He writes, *"I appeal to you for my child, Onesimus, whose father I became in my imprisonment."* When Paul uses this phrase about becoming Onesimus' father, we know he doesn't mean it in a literal way, but rather, in a spiritual way.

We see Peter using this same concept in 1 Peter 5:13 by calling Mark, *"my son."* John mentions followers of Christ as his children in 1 John 2:1, 12–13. And Paul refers to Timothy as *"my true son in the faith,"* thereby showing his close bond to Timothy in 1 Timothy 1:2.

In these three supporting examples, we have clear evidence that the apostles utilized this view of being "spiritual fathers" in connection to those whom they brought to the faith.

When Paul was making his appeal to Philemon, he is letting Philemon know this isn't just some ordinary appeal. This is a special appeal because Onesimus is a part of the family of God now. And Paul is acting in the role of his spiritual father. Paul understands something about a spiritual pedigree that he hopes to communicate to his Colossian friend. And that is this: Just as people develop inherited and acquired traits, we also develop spiritual traits. What kind of traits? Traits such as forgiveness, leadership, servanthood, and unity.

But where do we learn these traits from? Where can we best gain a visual of these traits in action? Usually from our leaders, teachers, and parents. That's what Paul is getting at here. Meaning that if you're a parent or in some type of Christian leadership, people are looking to you for guidance on how to live out this Christian experience best. Parenting and leadership carry influence by the nature of the roles. So, let's influence those we're accountable for in a way that is honoring to the Lord. That's what Paul is getting at here. And when we do, it will be a delightful pedigree for sure.

So, what happened to Onesimus? Well, we're not 100% certain, but history seems to indicate through the letters of St. Ignatius of Antioch and other church fathers that Philemon ended up taking Paul's advice and forgiving Onesimus. Philemon granted his freedom and encouraged Onesimus to return to Paul in Rome, as indicated in verse 21. Fifty years following this series of events, we catch up to Onesimus as he is mentioned in a letter to the church in Ephesus as a bishop of that congregation. From a slave to a bishop, what a journey! Paul's lesson to us is simple. Forgiveness not only frees us from the bondage of resentment, but also has the potential of releasing those we forgive into all that God has in store for them.

Conclusion

We began this chapter by looking at the compelling story of Onesimus and Philemon. We learned that Paul, as the spiritual leader, could have demanded Philemon to forgive his brother in the Lord, but instead of demanding, Paul encouraged Philemon to understand and receive the benefits of freely forgiving one who has wronged him. We discovered that forgiveness is powerful because it's deeply personal, is embedded in a divine principle, and carries a delightful pedigree. We also tackled five questions concerning forgiveness based on other passages of Scripture.

Questions such as...
- Who and what should we forgive?

Freedom

- How often should we forgive?
- Why should we forgive?
- What's the result when we forgive?
- What happens if we don't?

Yet through all of this, if you have yet to receive forgiveness from God through Christ for your sin, it will be next to impossible to put this powerful principle of forgiveness in place in your life.

There's a story about how Abraham Lincoln went to a slave auction one day and was appalled at what he saw. He was drawn to a young woman on the auction block. The bidding began, and Lincoln bid until he purchased her—no matter the cost. After he paid the auctioneer, he walked over to the woman and said, "You're free."

"Free? What is that supposed to mean?" she asked. "It means you are free," Lincoln answered, "completely free!" "Does it mean I can do whatever I want to do?" "Yes," he said, "free to do whatever you want to do." "Free to say whatever I want to say?" "Yes, free to say whatever you want to say." "Does freedom mean," asking with hope and hesitation, "that I can go wherever I want to go?"

"It means exactly that you can go wherever you want to go." With tears of joy and gratitude welling up in her eyes, she said, "Then, I think I'll go with you."[79]

"So, if the Son sets you free, you will be free indeed." (John 8:36)

T.K. Anderson

Finale

In writing this volume, the main hope is to be an encouragement to the Body of Christ. The entire world has recently come out of some very interesting and increasingly challenging times. And I'm not certain if things are going to get easier or more difficult for believers. However, if we're going to make it through all of this, we must learn to stick together. This thought reminds me of a somewhat humorous story.

There was a sailor and a land lover who went out fishing one day. The land lover hooked a great big fish. As he reeled it in, it was so heavy that it began to pull the ship itself. Suddenly, the fish made one last surge for freedom, and pulled the land lover overboard. Being a land lover, he couldn't swim a stroke. As he was trying to hold on to the fish, and coming up for air, he began to scream for help. "Help! I can't swim." The sailor, wanting to get him back into the ship, reached over the side, and grabbed him by the hair of his head, and, wouldn't you know it, he wore a wig. The wig came off, down he went, and the sailor grabbed an arm. You guessed it - an artificial arm - it came off. So, he reached out and grabbed the land lovers' leg, and it too was an artificial leg. It came off. The guy came up for the last time, crying, "Save me, I'm drowning." The sailor replied, "I would if you would stick together."

This story has a myriad of applications, but the main point for us is to remember that we don't have to go through life alone. Through all of our struggles, all of our hang-ups, all of our tribulations, and trials, know that we don't have to face it alone. As a local pastor, I must encourage you to get plugged into a local church if you haven't done so already. The importance of being connected during these days cannot be overemphasized enough. Especially with the thought that what we're facing today may be only the birth pangs of what's to come.

I love the local church because Jesus loves the local church. We are the hands and feet of our Savior to our communities. There are people uniquely designed for only you to reach. I cannot reach them, your pastor cannot reach them, someone else will not be able to impact their life, but God has designed you to be the one. That's the goal of this volume.

I hope you begin to experience the freedom that God provides as you learn to overcome your difficulties and begin to operate in the way God designed you to be. He loves you and wants you to soar in your relationship with Him. A circumstance that looks like it will knock you out can be the very circumstance that lifts you up. That's the message of this book, that's the message of Paul's life, that's the message of the Bible.

- Adam and Eve thought it was over when they disobeyed God, but God created a new plan.
- Noah thought the entire world would end, but God created a shelter of redemption through the ark.
- Abraham thought his promised son would be taken back, but God provided a last-minute rescue.
- Joseph thought his life was over in the pit, but God had plans for him to be in the palace.
- Moses thought the Red Sea was the end of the line, but God opened the waters and drown his enemies.
- David ran for his life from Saul, and all the while, God was preparing the way for a new kingdom.

Freedom

- Peter thought his ministry was over when he denied Christ three times, but Jesus thought a lakeside breakfast would be the perfect place for a restoration.
- Paul thought he was tainted and not qualified to be an apostle, but God thought he was the perfect guy to bring His message of love to the Gentiles.

Throughout the Bible we see time and again where people thought it was over, but God was just getting started. Where people saw a problem, God saw a plan. Where situations appeared overwhelming, God saw an opportunity. That's how God works!

I don't know what you're facing today, or what you've been going through, but I can say the same God who delivers, redeems, and sets people free throughout the pages of Scripture is the same God that can do it for you. Your situation is not shattering. Your failure is not final. Your circumstance is not catastrophic. You can experience true freedom as you allow Christ to work in you and through your circumstance, no matter the outcome.

Many of us are familiar with the 1957 motion picture, *The Bridge over the River Kwai*, starring Alec Guinness. It was selected as one of the 100 great films of the 20th century. It is the story of a group of British prisoners of war during World War II held by the Japanese in northern Burma in very difficult circumstances.

Ernest Gordon, a chaplain at Yale University, wrote a book called, *Through the River of the Kwai*, which shared his experience as a prisoner in that camp. It is a story of testing, hostility, and inspiration.

Gordon says that when the young soldiers in camp realized that they were going to be there for a while, they began to have Bible studies and to pray diligently that they would be delivered from their circumstances much as Israel prayed for deliverance from Rome. He said that at first their praying for deliverance was shallow and superficial. They railed against God for letting them be in that situation.

As time went on, however, something happened and their railing against God disappeared. They began to move toward more mature faith. They began to pray about their relations with one another. No longer was it "Why God?" but "How should we act, God?"

Gordon said the most spiritual moment of that experience was Christmas, 1944. Out of deference to the holiday, the men were not given work detail that day and were given a bit more food. He said that as they moved around the prison yard, they sensed that things were somehow different. In one of the barracks (basically a thatched hut with a dirt floor and open sides where the men slept), one soldier began to sing a Christmas carol. It was echoed over the infirmary where men were dying. Then all around the camp, the men began to sing, and those who could, those who were ambulatory, came to the parade field and sat there in a great circle. Gordon said, "God touched us that day."

He called it the most sacred event that he had ever been involved with. No preaching, nothing of the usual church equipment, just men united by their common misery, singing of God being with them and God's sovereignty. And he said, "We were touched by God."

That's my prayer for you, friend, as you spend time with God no

Freedom

matter your circumstance, that you'll be touched by God!

Let me leave you with a wonderful story from Acts 16:16-34. I've read this story many times as I've faced difficult situations over the years. Each time it has encouraged me to remember the very situation holding me down can be the very instrument God uses to work a miracle in the life of those around me.

"They grabbed Paul and Silas and dragged them before the authorities at the marketplace. [20] "The whole city is in an uproar because of these Jews!" they shouted to the city officials. [21] "They are teaching customs that are illegal for us Romans to practice."

[22] A mob quickly formed against Paul and Silas, and the city officials ordered them stripped and beaten with wooden rods. [23] They were severely beaten, and then they were thrown into prison. The jailer was ordered to make sure they didn't escape. [24] So the jailer put them into the inner dungeon and clamped their feet in the stocks.

[25] Around midnight Paul and Silas were praying and singing hymns to God, and the other prisoners were listening. [26] Suddenly, there was a massive earthquake, and the prison was shaken to its foundations. All the doors immediately flew open, and the chains of every prisoner fell off! [27] The jailer woke up to see the prison doors wide open. He assumed the prisoners had escaped, so he drew his sword to kill himself. [28] But Paul shouted to him, "Stop! Don't kill yourself! We are all here!"

[29] The jailer called for lights and ran to the dungeon and fell down trembling before Paul and Silas. [30] Then he brought them out and asked, "Sirs, what must I do to be saved?"

³¹ They replied, "Believe in the Lord Jesus and you will be saved, along with everyone in your household." ³² And they shared the word of the Lord with him and with all who lived in his household.

³³ Even at that hour of the night, the jailer cared for them and washed their wounds. Then he and everyone in his household were immediately baptized. ³⁴ He brought them into his house and set a meal before them, and he and his entire household rejoiced because they all believed in God.[80]

About the Author

T.K. Anderson has served in pastoral ministry for over two decades. He is passionate about teaching the Word of God, using apologetics to answer the questions that often go unasked. He is the author of three books, including *Pocket Theology* and *Faith Jump*. He holds a bachelor's degree in Theological Studies from North Central University, a master's degree in Christian Apologetics from Biola University and is completing his D.Min. at Southern California Seminary. Mr. Anderson holds dual memberships with the Evangelical Theological and Philosophical Societies. He currently serves as the Lead Pastor of **Compass Church** in Salinas, CA.

ENDNOTES

[1] Accessed, February 18, 2021, https://www.beliefnet.com/columnists/leavingsalem/2011/12/is-there-any-hope.html
[2] Source: *Gold Mines in North Carolina,* John Hairr & Joey Powell
[3] Philemon 1:9, Ephesians 3:1, Philippians 1:12-14, Colossians 4:18
[4] Accessed February 18, 2021, https://daily-dew.com/shaved-by-grace
[5] Source: *View from the Cockpit,* Archie B. Lawson
[6] Accessed February 8, 2021, https://ministry127.com/resources/illustration/a-w-tozer-on-grace
[7] Jeremiah Study Bible (ESV), Ephesians, 1592.
[8] Our Daily Bread
[9] Source: USAToday.com, December 3, 2012
[10] Source: Ocala Star-Banner, September 1, 2004
[11] Holman N.T. Commentary on Ephesians, Max Anders
[12] The Jeremiah Study Bible, Ephesians 3:6, 1596.
[13] Accessed February 2, 2021, https://ministry127.com/resources/illustration/avoiding-pitfalls
[14] Dr. David Jeremiah, *A Life Beyond Amazing* (Nashville: Thomas Nelson, 2017) 12.
[15] Accessed February 9, 2021, https://www.cnn.com/2007/POLITICS/10/22/murphy.medal.of.honor/index.html?_s=PM:POLITICS
[16] Orel Hershiser, *Out of the Blue* (Wolgemuth & Hyatt, 1989)
[17] Adapted from the Jeremiah Study Bible (ESV) Ephesians 4:1, 1597.
[18] https://www.blueletterbible.org/lang/lexicon/lexicon.cfm?Strongs=G4239&t=ESV
[19] Jeremiah Study Bible (ESV), Ephesians 4:3, 1597.
[20] *The Pursuit of God,* A.W. Tozer
[21] https://www.biblegateway.com/passage/?search=John+4&version=ESV
[22] Ibid.
[23] https://www.pbs.org/wgbh/americanexperience/features/light-introduction/
[24] Jeremiah Study Bible (ESV), Ephesians 6:12-18, 1601.
[25] https://www.blueletterbible.org/Comm/guzik_david/StudyGuide2017-Eph/Eph-6.cfm?a=1103010
[26] https://www.gotquestions.org/what-is-a-psalm.html
[27] https://ministry127.com/resources/illustration/2-oranges-and-an-agnostic
[28] https://en.wikipedia.org/wiki/The_Heavenly_Vision
[29] Source: Nightlights for Students, Jim Fletcher, Roger Howerton
[30] https://www.brainyquote.com/quotes/george_s_patton_104742
[31] A Life Beyond Amazing, Dr. David Jeremiah, Thomas Nelson, 2017. ix.
[32] https://ministry127.com/resources/illustration/christ-is-our-representative
[33] Accessed, March 3, 2021, https://www.cybersalt.org/clean-jokes/bricklayers-insurance-claim
[34] Accessed 3/17/21, https://www.christianquotes.info/quotes-by-topic/quotes-about-adversity/
[35] Accessed 3/17/21, https://www.goodreads.com/quotes/514597-comfort-and-prosperity-have-never-enriched-the-world-as-much
[36] Accessed March 24, 2021, https://ministry127.com/resources/illustration/pulling-an-airplane
[37] Accessed March 24, 2021, https://groovyhistory.com/agony-of-defeat-wide-world-of-sports-vinko-bogataj
[38] Accessed, April 11, 2021, https://treecutpros.com/fastest-growing-trees-in-the-world/
[39] Accessed, April 11, 2021, https://www.giant-sequoia.com/faqs/giant-sequoia-landscape-questions/
[40] Psalms 16:11 (ESV), accessed July 14, 2021, https://esv.literalword.com
[41] Accessed July 14, 2021, https://www.americamagazine.org/issue/culture/life-after-life-after-death
[42] Accessed July 14, 2021, https://ministry127.com/resources/illustration/refining-silver. Source: The Mother's Magazine, Volume 3, A. G. Whittelsey
[43] Accessed, July 19, 2021, https://ministry127.com/resources/illustration/the-wisdom-of-silence
[44] Accessed, July 19, 2021, https://www.psychologytoday.com/us/blog/evolution-the-self/201609/8-crucial-differences-between-healthy-and-unhealthy-pride
[45] Accessed August 7, 2021, https://www.christianquotes.info/images/b-simpson-quote-gods-boundless-resources
[46] J. Vernon McGee, Through the Bible with J. Vernon McGee (Nashville: Thomas Nelson; 1984).
[47] Accessed, August 7, 2021, https://genius.com/Horatio-spafford-it-is-well-lyrics#about
[48] Accessed September 1st, 2021, https://ofhsoupkitchen.org/empathy-quotes

[49] Accessed September 1st, 2021, https://en.wikipedia.org/wiki/He%27s_Got_the_Whole_World_in_His_Hands
[50] Accessed, July 19, 2021, https://ministry127.com/resources/illustration/superman-and-muhammad-ali
[51] Accessed, September 8, 2021, https://www.pewresearch.org/internet/2021/04/07/social-media-use-in-2021
[52] Accessed, August 23, 2021, https://www.foxnews.com/sports/tom-brady-disavows-work-ethic
[53] Accessed, September 8, 2021, https://billygraham.org/answer/christians-should-be-joyful-people
[54] David Jeremiah Study Bible, Worthy Publishing: New York, NY. Page 1612.
[55] Accessed September 10, 2021, https://www.gotquestions.org/garment-of-praise.html
[56] Accessed September 10, 2021, https://awakeusnowministries.com/blog/2020/11/07/day-36-40-days-of-prayer-for-america
[57] Accessed, March 1, 2021, https://www.sermoncentral.com/sermon-illustrations/9425/heaven-by-stephan-brown
[58] David Jeremiah, Count it all Joy, 174.
[59] Accessed October 3, 2021, https://www.blueletterbible.org/lexicon/g1901/esv/mgnt/0-1/
[60] Accessed October 3, 2021, https://www.goodreads.com/quotes/76039-do-you-know-why-the-nose-of-the-bull-dog
[61] Accessed March 1, 2021, http://vincelombardi.com/number-one.html
[62] Accessed, March 1, 2021, https://www.sermoncentral.com/sermon-illustrations/100272/heaven-by-paul-steen
[63] Accessed, March 1, 2021, http://www.moreillustrations.com/Illustrations/race.html
[64] https://thesaker.is/alexander-solzhenitsyns-harvard-address/
[65] Ericson, Edward E. Jr. (October 1985) "Solzhenitsyn – Voice from the Gulag,"
[66] https://thirdmill.org/seminary/lesson.asp/vid/18
[67] https://nypost.com/2020/01/23/these-are-the-top-30-most-recognizable-logos-in-the-usa/
[68] Ron Hutchcraft, Wake Up Calls, Moody, 1990, p. 22.
[69] https://www.baag.in/trees-with-the-deepest-and-longest-roots-in-the-world/ accessed September 14, 2022
[70] https://freeccm.com/2018/03/06/behind-the-song-hillsong-united-shares-the-heart-behind-their-single-so-will-i-100-billion-x/
[71] https://tonycooke.org/stories-and-illustrations/johnny-duck/
[72] Fred Brown, "Hancock Moonshiner Was 'Catchable But Not Fetchable,'" the Knoxville News-Sentinel, July 22, 1990, Section B, pp. 1, 6
[73] https://zcrcimus.org/library/sermons/the-chief-end-of-man
[74] Accessed April 12, 2022; msn.com article dated June 3, 2011.
[75] Accessed May 9, 2021, https://en.wikipedia.org/wiki/Christopher_Gadsden
[76] Accessed, May 9, 2021, https://historyplex.com/the-boston-tea-party
[77] Accessed May 10, 2021, https://www1.cbn.com/cbnnews/healthscience/2015/June/The-Deadly-Consequences-of-Unforgiveness
[78] Accessed, May 21, 2021, https://www.latimes.com/archives/la-xpm-2000-jun-28-sp-45555-story.html
[79] https://www.kevinhalloran.net/abraham-lincoln-christian-faith-slavery-and-gods-grace/
[80] *Holy Bible*, New Living Translation, copyright © 1996, 2004, 2015 by Tyndale House Foundation. Used by permission of Tyndale House Publishers, Inc., Carol Stream, Illinois 60188. All rights reserved.

Made in the USA
Middletown, DE
04 November 2022